Intelligent Guides to Wines

Southwest France

2021 Edition

Benjamin Lewin MW

ISBN: 9781980733836

Vendange Press

www.vendangepress.com

Preface

This Guide is devoted specifically to the Southwest, in particular the two general areas of Bergerac-Cahors-Gaillac, and Madiran-Jurançon. The guide is divided into two parts. The first part of the guide discusses the regions, and explains the character and range of the wines. The second part profiles the producers. There are detailed profiles of the leading producers, showing how each winemaker interprets the local character.

In the first part I address the nature of the wines made today and ask how this has changed, how it's driven by tradition or competition, and how styles may evolve in the future. I show how the wines are related to the terroir and to the types of grape varieties that are grown, and I explain the classification system. For each region, I suggest reference wines that I believe typify the area; in some cases, where there is a split between, for example, modernists and traditionalists, there may be wines from each camp.

In the second part, there's no single definition for what constitutes a top producer. Leading producers range from those who are so prominent as to represent the common public face of an appellation to those who demonstrate an unexpected potential on a tiny scale. The producers profiled in the guide represent the best of both tradition and innovation in wine in the region. In each profile, I have tried to give a sense of the producer's aims for his wines, of the personality and philosophy behind them—to meet the person who makes the wine, as it were, as much as to review the wines themselves.

Each profile shows a sample label, a picture of the winery, and details of production, followed by a description of the producer and winemaker. Each producer is rated (from one to four stars). For each producer I suggest reference wines that are a good starting point for understanding the style. Most of the producers welcome visits, although some require appointments: details are in the profiles. Profiles are organized geographically, and each group of profiles is preceded by maps showing the locations of producers to help plan itineraries.

The guide is based on many visits to France over recent years. I owe an enormous debt to the many producers who cooperated in this venture by engaging in discussion and opening innumerable bottles for tasting. This guide would not have been possible without them.

Benjamin Lewin

Contents

Tables

Appellation Maps

Producer Maps

Overview of the Southwest

The Southwest is a real grab bag of regions, including everything between Bordeaux and the Languedoc. The wide variety of terroirs and climatic variation results in many different wine styles. The region really falls into two distinct parts: Bordeaux satellites; and the far Southwest (near the Pyrenees).

If there's one single word that describes the dominant character of the red wines of the entire Southwest, it is: tannin. This reflects the character of Malbec, once a dominant grape in Bordeaux, and today grown only in the area immediately to its southeast, and Tannat, the most important black grape of the Pyrenees. Both have a natural tendency to very high tannins. The reds are powerful; the traditional varieties stand up to the heat well, but the key to red winemaking in the southwest is taming the powerful tannins.

Dry white wine has been something of a struggle, and the best known whites are the sweet wines. In the Bordeaux satellites, these come from the same varieties as Bordeaux, with an emphasis on complexity coming from botrytis. In the Pyrenees, they come from the more aromatic varie-

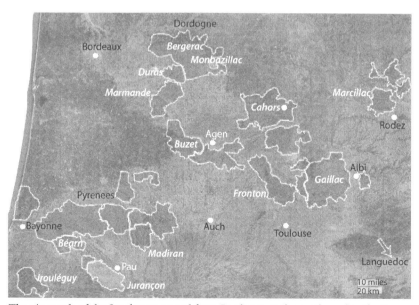

The vineyards of the Southwest extend from Bordeaux at the north, and to the Pyrenees at the south. To the southeast is the Languedoc.

ties of Petit and Gros Manseng, with passerillage (desiccation on the vine) as the means of achieving concentration.

The production of sweet wines all over the southwest makes the point that this is a hot climate extending into autumn. It's not always obvious that the dry reds, dry whites, and sweet whites come from the same areas, because different appellation names may be used for each style (sometimes Sec is used to distinguish dry wine), but the fact is that this is a region with a Continental climate inclining to strong temperature transitions.

The region has a concentration of indigenous varieties that are grown nowhere else; indeed, there may be more unusual varieties here than in the rest of France combined: Duras, Fer Servadou, Prunelart black varieties and Len d'El, Mauzac and Ondenc white varieties in Gaillac; the Mansengs and Courbu in Jurançon and Irouléguy whites.

The Dordogne

There's a story that a tourist asked the tourism office in Bordeaux to recommend vineyards to visit in the Dordogne. "There are no vineyards in the Dordogne," was the reply. In fact, the winegrowing regions of the Dordogne are just to the southeast of Bordeaux; started by the Romans, winegrowing here actually preceded production in Bordeaux. Before phylloxera, wine was grown widely in the area, and shipped along the river to be exported through Bordeaux. After the Middle Ages, Bergerac suffered by comparison with Bordeaux not because its wines were inferior, but because protectionism favored the export of local wines from Bordeaux. After phylloxera, vineyards retreated to the area around Bergerac itself.

The distinction between this region and Bordeaux was not always so clear. When the zone for the wines of Bordeaux was first specified in 1909, it included many communes in the Dordogne and in Lot-et-Garonne. Protests from Bordeaux caused the region to be limited strictly to the department of the Gironde, so the area had to develop its own identity.

Wine is no longer the main focus of the region, which has shifted to tourism. At its peak, there were 18,000 hectares of vines; a revival in recent years has brought the total back up to over 12,000. Some growers feel that the problem is the dominance of cooperatives and negociants from Bordeaux who buy the wine to make cheap brands.

The mix of grape varieties and the range of wines are similar to Bordeaux. Grapes reach ripeness later, with harvest usually about ten days after Bordeaux, so the style is not so ripe. Red wine predominates, and there are both dry and sweet white wines. Bergerac (for dry wines) and Monbazillac (for sweet wines) are the best known appellations.

Bergerac & Monbazillac

The AOP of Bergerac covers the entire region. The majority of production is red or rosé. Bergerac Sec describes dry white wine. In addition to Monbazillac, there are also some smaller appellations within Bergerac AOP, including Montravel, Pécharmant (red only), and Saussignac and Rosette (very small AOPs for sweet white wines). Most of the sweet whites are moelleux, where the sweetness comes from desiccation of the grapes. Liquoreux (botrytized) wines come from specific appellations.

The tradition in the area is to use different names for different styles of wines. So while Bergerac refers to dry wines, Côtes de Bergerac is used for sweet wines coming from anywhere in the area. In the same way, Montravel is a small area at the western border, where Montravel AOP is

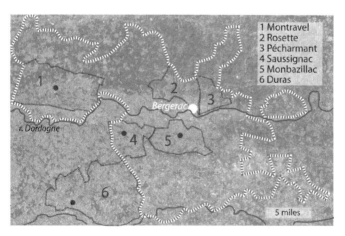

Bergerac AOP extends north and south of the river Dordogne around the town of Bergerac. Bergerac Sec covers the same area for dry white wine. Côtes de Bergerac is not a separate area but a description for moelleux (sweet) white wine; it can also be used for red wines that reach a higher quality standard than Bergerac. Pécharmant, Monbazillac, Saussignac, Rosette, and Montravel (including Haut Montravel and Côtes de Montravel) are AOPs within Bergerac.

AOPs in Bergerac			
AOP	Wines	Ha	Growers
Bergerac	red, rosé, dry white (40%)	12,800	1,200
Côtes de Bergerac	red, dry white & sweet (moelleux)		
Montravel	red & dry white (85%)	250	24
Haut Montravel	sweet (botrytized)	50	14
Côtes de Montravel	sweet (moelleux)	50	14
Monbazillac	sweet (moelleux or botrytized)	2,360	144
Pécharmant	red	420	50
Rosette	sweet (moelleux)	44	16
Saussignac	sweet (botrytized)	33	23

for dry wines, Côtes de Montravel is for sweet white in the moelleux category, and Haut Montravel is for liquoreux (botrytized) wines. Franck Pascal at Domaine du Jonc Blanc summarizes how he labels his wines. "If the white has less than 3 grams of residual sugar, it is Bergerac Sec. Between 3 and 9g, it's Vin de France; 9-20g is Côtes de Montravel and more than 20 grams becomes Côtes de Bergerac."

Although reds are often based on Merlot, they don't have the generosity of the right bank of Bordeaux, but convey a slightly harder, sometimes more rustic impression. There's quite a bit of Cabernet Sauvignon and Malbec; Cabernet Franc is less evident. As they age, the reds often develop notes of truffles to contrast with the fruits. It can be difficult to get the right balance between softening the wines (at risk of losing character) and keeping so much tannin that aging is required (which may not be so appropriate for Bergerac as for Bordeaux).

The red is undergoing a bit of an identity crisis. Attempts at modernization lead to soft almost furry tannins, but the rustic character remains in the background. In terms of comparison with Bordeaux, the best wines are closest in style to the Côtes de Castillon.

In an attempt to improve quality, a higher level appellation called Côtes de Bergerac was introduced. Confusingly, this is the same term used for the moelleux white wines. Yields are limited to 50 hl/ha compared to 60 hl/ha for Bergerac, and chaptalization is forbidden. But it's only 4% of the production of Bergerac. There's some talk about calling it Grand Cru instead of Côtes. While Bergerac AOP is usually aged in cuve. Côtes de Bergerac reds often age in barriques.

Pécharmant (which means charming hill), just northeast of Bergerac, is often considered to produce the best red wines of the area from terroir of sand and gravel over iron-rich clay, known locally as 'tran'.

Bergerac Sec tends to show a perfumed quality, with stone fruits of apricots and peaches rather than citrus, turning in a more savory direction than you find with white Bordeaux. It's usually a blend of Sauvignon Blanc with Sémillon.

Sweet wine is made through the whole area. The top area for sweet wine is Monbazillac, from a favored area where botrytis is more common, although less consistent than Sauternes. Emphasizing the difference between the requirements for producing sweet versus dry wine, the vineyards in Monbazillac tend to face north, where fogs develop best, as opposed to facing south to catch the sun. Wines can come from a mixture of botrytized berries, some passerillé, and some very mature berries, and can vary from moelleux (medium sweet) to liquoreux (fully sweet).

Varieties for the sweet wines are similar to Sauternes, with Sémillon as the driving force, but there tends to be somewhat more Muscadelle in Monbazillac, which may contribute to a more perfumed note. Quality and reputation declined in the late twentieth century, when vineyards were planted at lower densities, mechanical harvesting was introduced, and there was much chaptalization. In the past twenty years, however, there has been a revival.

Monbazillac in the hands of an average producer can appear to be a poor man's Sauternes. But from a top producer, such as Tirecul La Gravière, it displays its own character, more savory, with herbal overtones running to anise providing a counterpoise to the sweetness. Aromas of truffles are common on the sweet wines, and intensify after a few years. The very best wines come into their own after a decade and continue to develop for another decade or so.

A new label, SGN, has been introduced for the top Monbazillacs: it requires 17% potential alcohol (compared with 14% for Monbazillac), maturation for 18 months, and chaptalization is forbidden. Essentially this is a wine based on full botrytis. Sweet wines from Saussignac also are usually botrytized.

Immediately to the south of Montravel, the Côtes de Duras is another Bordeaux satellite—considered part of the Haut Pays Bordelais in the Middle Ages—making red wine from Bordeaux varieties and white wine from Bordeaux varieties with some more southern varieties.

South of Duras, the Côtes de Marmandais has a more Continental climate, producing mostly red wine from mostly Bordeaux varieties dominated by Merlot. Other varieties that are allowed include Syrah, Fer Servadou, Malbec, and Gamay, and a variety that is almost unique to Marmandais, Abouriou. Almost all production goes through the cooperative.

Cahors

Moving another fifty miles east and a bit south, imagine a triangle with Cahors at the apex, and Fronton and Gaillac at its base to the south. Malbec, once a dominant grape in Bordeaux but no longer much grown there, is a major variety in Cahors. Cahors AOP is exclusively red. Fronton is probably the only place in France that grows the Negrette grape. Gaillac, a very old established area for wine production, is the last place growing Len de l'El, Mauzac, and Ondenc.

Cahors was famous in the Middle Ages for its wine. During the fourteenth century, half the wine shipped out of Bordeaux came from the region around Cahors. It was known for the so-called 'black wine of Cahors.' Originally this described a preparation made by heating the must before fermentation, which was then used to strengthen weaker wines, but then it came to refer to the wine generally, which is indeed very deeply colored. It remained famous until the vineyards were wiped out by phylloxera in the nineteenth century.

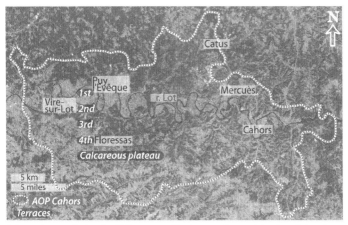

Most vineyards in the Cahors appellation are located in the plain along the river. Terraces dating from different geological eras rise up to the south.

The problem after phylloxera was that Malbec did not graft well onto the available rootstocks, so producers were forced into planting inferior varieties. The revival started after the frost of 1956 wiped out many vineyards, and replanting started with new clones , but interest did not really pick up until the success of Argentina with Malbec brought the grape back into fashion. Since 2007 the modern approach has been encouraged by allowing 'Malbec' to be stated on the label.

Vineyards in Cahors occupy something of an oval around the river Lot, with the town of Cahors at one end. Soils are mostly based on clay and chalk, although there are some places with a very high iron content, where the soil is quite red. As Cahors is more or less equidistant from the Atlantic, the Mediterranean, and the Pyrenees, the climate can be cooler in years driven by the maritime influence from the west, or warmer in years when the weather comes from the south. Frost has been a problem in recent vintages, with 80% of the crop lost in 2017, and 60-70% in 2019.

The most important producers are concentrated around the town of Vire-sur-Lot. There are vineyards on the flat and on a series of terraces running up to the woods. The terraces are the defining geographical feature, representing different geological ages and types of limestone. Producers' views vary as to whether to reflect different terraces in different cuvées, as at Clos Triguedina or Cosse Maisonneuve, or whether to try for more complexity by blending, as at Château de Cèdre.

Soils become increasingly less fertile moving up from the flat area near the river, through the terraces, to the plateau at the top. And the farther up from the river, the more limestone there is in the soil. The first terrace, by the river, has alluvial soils. and produces wines that tend to be

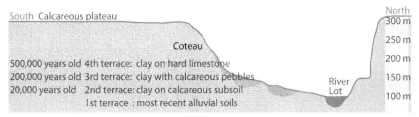

Terraces dating from different geological eras rise up to the south as seen in a cross-section view. The second terrace is clay on top of calcareous subsoil, giving fruitiness. The third terrace has clay with round pebbles and calcareous subsoils, giving richness. The fourth terrace is clay on hard limestone, giving finesse and elegance. The calcareous plateau is Kimmeridgian.

fruity and forward, and meant to be enjoyed young. The second terrace has clay with some limestone, and the wines are still relatively forward. The wines are more powerful and longer-lived from the third and fourth terraces, which become stony with hard limestone.

There's an increasing tendency to make wines from the plateau at the top, the Plateau Calcaire or Causses as it's called locally, where the soil is thin clay on top of Kimmeridgian limestone with iron-rich red and blue clay. Parts of the plateau have the unique sidérolithique terroir, consisting of clay and sandstone with a high iron content. The altitude on the plateau ranges from 250-350m. The wines tend to a more mineral character. Some new growers have set up on the plateau and are setting a standard for elegance and refinement.

Although the grape major grape variety is Malbec, the dominant stylistic influence is Bordeaux, albeit not as obviously as in Bergerac where the grape varieties are Bordelais. Malbec is known locally as Côt, or also as Auxerrois (no connection with the white grape of Alsace with the same name). Malbec is not so dominant as when this was known as the 'black wine', but must still comprise at least 70% of the blend in Cahors. The rest is usually Merlot.

The tendency is for entry-level and intermediate wines to be blends, but for top wines to be 100% Malbec. Usually entry-level wines are aged in concrete to tame tannins and preserve fruits, a proportion of oak is introduced into the intermediate level, and the top wines are often aged in barriques.

Catherine Maisonneuve makes four different Malbecs from different positions on the slope. Why are they 100% Malbec? "Merlot has been here only for 60 years; they authorized Merlot because they had planted Malbec in the 1960s that was too productive, but it's the Malbec that expresses the terroir," she says.

The same effect of increasingly refined character going up the slope is seen here and in the Trilogie of wines from successive terraces at Clos Triguedina, where Jean-Luc Baldès explains: "Malbec can bring finesse and elegance, it does not need to be massive, it can be fresh and mineral. Our problem is that the image of Cahors in the 1980s was for a rather rustic wine. The success of Argentina opened the door to making another style of wine. Our objective is to show the refinement and elegance of Malbec."

The Malbec that Argentina has made its principal black variety came from Cahors, of course, after production there was destroyed by phyllox-

Local Grape Varieties from Cahors-Madiran	
Cahors	
Malbec	Formerly grown in Bordeaux, now grown in significant amounts only in Cahors, where it must be at least 70% of the blend. The wine is dark and tannic: even with modern methods, it usually requires time.
Gaillac	
Fer Servadou	Also known as *Braucol* or *Verdot,* is a relatively tannic, dark-skinned variety, with a tendency to rusticity. It's most prominent in Marcillac (about 40 miles east of Cahors), where it must be at least 90% of the blend, but small amounts are included in the blend in Gaillac, Madiran, and Fronton.
Mauzac	High-acid white variety, often with a taste of green apples, and the main variety for the sparkling Blanquette de Limoux in Languedoc. It also makes sparkling and still wine in Gaillac.
L'El de l'El	White variety of Gaillac, often blended with Mauzac or Ondenc. It has relatively low acidity and is often a component in late-harvest, sweet wines. The name is probably a contraction of *Loin de l'Oeil.*
Ondenc	Once grown in the Loire, Cognac, and Armagnac, but now found only in Gaillac, because low yields and susceptibility to rot meant it was not replanted after phylloxera. It's often a component in late-harvest, sweet wines.
Fronton	
Negrette	Small barries in tight bunches have dark color, but are low in tannins and acidity, so ften blended with strong varieties such as Cabernet Sauvignon or Syrah. Now grown only in Fronton (west of Gaillac), where wines must have at least 50% Negrette.
Madiran	
Tannat	One of the most tannic grape varieties grown in France. Micro-oxygenation is often used to soften the wine, but it usually requires several years to soften.

era at the end of the nineteenth century. More recently the compliment has been returned, with Argentine winemakers now taking an interest in Cahors. Mendoza producer Altos Las Hormigos has established a collaboration with Métairie Grande du Théron, Château les Croisille, and Domaine du Prince in Cahors. The objective is to make wines reflecting limestone terroirs.

At its best, Malbec can indeed be quite refined, without either the overt fleshiness of Merlot or the bare bones structure of Cabernet. The problem is that the best examples are wines where, even if the tannins are fine, they are still quite present when young. There are now second wines made in a more fruity and approachable style, but in my opinion, even if Cahors is no longer the impenetrable black wine of the past, it still always needs at least five years after the vintage before you can see the fruits clearly and enjoy them. It is just the DNA of Malbec in this region.

Gaillac

Moving south and east towards Albi, Gaillac supports its claim to be one of the oldest sites for wine production in France by pointing to the existence of wild grapevines in the Grésigne forest near the river Tarn. Wine was made here during the Roman era, all but destroyed by the Moors during their occupation in the Middle Ages, and then revived by the monks, led by the Abbaye of Saint Michel, which developed a thriving export trade. The development of Gaillac and surrounding regions was impeded by the protectionism of the Bordelais, and it wasn't until the eve of the French Revolution that the wines of Gaillac could be sold freely.

Gaillac has an unusually wide range of grape varieties. In reds, the principal varieties include Duras and Fer Servadou, which are traditional varieties going back more than a century, and Syrah (introduced more recently): Gamay used to be allowed but has now been eliminated. All the Bordeaux varieties are permitted. Malbec, Tannat, and Negrette are also found. The traditional white varieties are Mauzac (both blanc and rosé), the curiously named l'En de l'El, Ondenc, and then the usual suspects from Bordeaux.

Wild grapevines grow in the forest of Grésigne. Courtesy IFV Sud-Ouest.

The debate in Gaillac as to whether the appellation should preserve the old varieties or represent the new has been won by the modernists. The authorities in Gaillac seem especially determined to stamp out individuality among

Reference Wines for Dordogne - Southwest	
Bergerac	Vignoble des Verdots
Bergerac Sec	Domaine l'Ancienne Cure
Cahors	Clos Triguedina
Gaillac	Domaine Plageoles Causse Marines
Monbazillac	Tirecul La Gravière

their producers, yet have no clear idea of what Gaillac should represent. It's a very curious view the appellation has of itself, that wines made from varieties as different as Braucol, Duras, or Syrah can be labeled as Gaillac; styles as different as dry white, semi-sweet white, vendange tardive (late harvest sweet) wines (since 2012), and vin de voile (an oxidized style grown under a layer of flor) can be labeled as Gaillac; even a sparkling wine made from the Mauzac grape: but varieties that were grown here two centuries ago aren't allowed, and producers who make low-sulfur wines are thrown out of the appellation because of supposed notes of oxidation.

So top producers, such as Plageoles, Patrice Lescarret at Causse Marines, and Michel Issaly, who have reintroduced some of the really old varieties, have to label the wines as Vins de France because the cépages aren't allowed in the appellation. Their rediscovery is due largely to Robert Plageoles, who recollects, "One day I realized, that's our heritage. It was a grand adventure to restart, to find the old varieties, but it was a long road, very lonely at first." Black grape varieties include Prunelart, Mauzac Noir, and Verdanel; whites include various subvarieties of Mauzac.

Tasting the old varieties leaves me with mixed feelings. They are definitely different from the international style, but they don't always offer enough distinctive flavor interest. Certainly it's easier to make wine to the general taste from the more common varieties. "My wines are completely atypical. No one would recognize them as Gaillac because there are very few vignerons left who work with authentic varieties. They are all using Merlot, Syrah, and Gamay. We are losing the appellation with the most distinctive set of varieties," says Michel Issaly.

The most authentic taste of Gaillac perhaps comes from the Vin de Voile, which is distinctive in tending to show more overt fruits than you see with either the Jura or Sherry. Some producers bottle it as a vintage (after seven years under the voile), some make multi-vintage blends, and Patrice Lescarret has a solera. "Vin de voile is different, it's the true history, wine like this gives the true impression of Gaillac. I believe this is the best wine you can make in Gaillac," says Michel Issaly.

To the west of Gaillac, Fronton has three soil types in terraces that rise up from the Tarn river. Close to the river, the first river has *boulbènes*, consisting of limestone and crushed quartz. The second terrace has iron-rich clay and silt. The highest terrace has gravel. As with Cahors, finesse increases going up the terraces. Fronton has only black grapes, with a high proportion of Negrette, another one of the southern grapes with high tannic content.

The Pyrenees

The wine-producing areas of the Pyrenees fall into two parts. To the north are a group of appellations in Gascony, where Madiran is the most distinguished. They are known best for firm red wines, although sweet wines are also a feature. Known for its powerful tannins, Tannat is the predominant black grape variety. It may be blended with Cabernet Franc or Cabernet Sauvignon.

To the south are the sweet wine region of Jurançon and the Basque region of Irouléguy, where the influence is as much Spanish as French. All across the Pyrenees, Petit and Gros Manseng are the dominant white varieties used for producing sweet wine; Courbu has declined because it's unproductive and does not do well in wet Spring seasons.

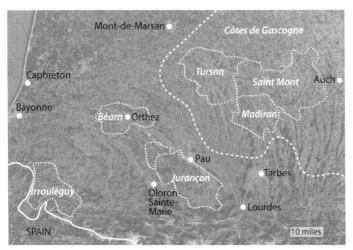

The vineyards of the Pyrenees extend from Gascony to the Spanish border. Madiran, Tursan, and Saint Mont are north of Pau and are surrounded by the IGP Côtes de Gascogne, which extends north towards the Dordogne. Jurançon, Béarn, and Irouléguy extend from Pau to the Pyrenees.

Madiran

Considered part of the Southwest, but completely different from the area between Bergerac and Cahors, the vineyards close to the Pyrenees show the influence of the Basque country. Madiran is famous for the strong Tannat grape that is the backbone of its red wine. Jurançon makes dry and sweet white wine from the Gros and Petit Manseng varieties. Irouléguy's vineyards are close to the border with Spain, just up against the Pyrenees, and also grow Tannat and the Mansengs.

Madiran covers five hills, with the best vineyards planted on slopes facing south or southeast. Elevation is an important factor in terroir: it's much drier on the hills where the sedimentary rocks become hot in summer; going down the slope, the soil turns to gravelly clay; and then there's more clay, and therefore better retention of moisture, in the valleys. Most plantings are on the middle slopes.

There's also variation across the appellation. Clay is the major soil-type, and differences in terroir are due to variations in the clay. The western part of the appellation is more or less pure clay. The slopes of Saint Lanne in the eastern part have clay mixed with iron and magnesium, giving the wines a more solid character. Around Maumusson, there's a concentration of the terroir known locally as sol à greppe, where there are slabs of limestone under the clay, and some sand and small rocks of

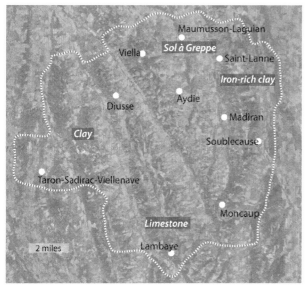

Madiran has clay everywhere. The most distinguished terroirs are in the northeast.

Tannat is a darkly colored, thick-skinned variety (inset). A small plot at Château Barréjat has pre-phylloxera vines, planted in pairs in the old style.

limestone make rounder wines. There's some limestone in the south.

Madiran is among the most powerful wines of France. Tannat is the traditional grape, although the proportion that is required or allowed has kept changing since the appellation was created. The last iteration specified between 40% and 80%, with Cabernet Sauvignon, Cabernet Franc, and Fer Servadou as the other varieties (none exactly known for softness). Some producers have settled on 'Tradition' as a label describing entry-level wines that are 80% Tannat with 20% Cabernet Franc or Cabernet Sauvignon, aged in cuve to focus on fruits. Whether formally allowed or not, the top wines are often 100% Tannat, usually aged in barriques, usually with one- or two-year or older oak rather than new.

The problem is that it's Scylla and Charybdis between becoming round, soft, jammy, and losing character, as against displaying the nature of Tannat, which inevitably means showing tannins. It's not just that the strong tannins take years to soften, but just as much that the fruit flavor spectrum tends to be monolithic: it takes about a decade before flavor variety develops. The high praise given to wines such as the prestige cuvées of Château Montus during their youth reflects potential for what will happen in another twenty years, more than present drinking pleasure. It's quite difficult to judge Madiran when it's young.

There are different opinions on how best to tame the tannins. Introduced by Patrick Ducournau in 1990, a popular approach is micro-oxygenation, which involves exposing the wine to a stream of tiny oxygen bubbles. This softens the tannins (technically it causes them to polymerize sooner), making the wine more approachable. However, the most important producer in Madiran, Alain Brumont (of Châteaux Bouscassé and Montus), is scathing about the technique "I have nothing to do with it," he says, "I buy new barrels and that provides quite sufficient oxygenation." Tannat needs oak to soften it. The problem with Tannat is that it's not very aromatic, and can lack freshness (which is why Cabernet is often included in the lower level cuvées).

Madiran is only red. The appellation white wine that's produced in the region goes under the name of Pacherenc du Vic-Bilh. The AOP covers exactly the same area as Madiran. Pacherenc du Vic-Bilh on the label means the wine is sweet: Pacherenc du Vic-Bilh Sec is used for dry white wine. The grapes are mostly Petit and Gros Manseng, with some Petit Corbu.

Jurançon

The great name for white wine in the region is Jurançon. This originated as an exclusively sweet wine, in the category called *moelleux*, which comes from late harvested grapes (as opposed to even sweeter *liquoreux* wines, which usually come from botrytized grapes). It can come from Petit or Gros Manseng, but the former is by far the finer, and dominates the top cuvées. It's about a quarter of all plantings. Petit Manseng is very susceptible to passerillage. In fact the grapes look pretty much as shriveled as botrytized grapes although there is no botrytis.

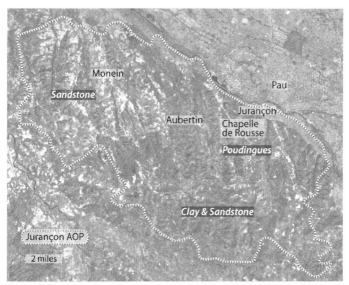

Jurançon has three general types of terroir.

White Grape Varieties of the Pyrenees	
Gros Manseng	Aromatic white variety that is a major grape in Jurançon, today used more for dry wine. Thick skin protects against rot, acidity is high, sugar levels are high. Overall impression can be rustic as monovarietal, and quality is improved by blending with Petit Manseng.
Petit Manseng	More refined than Gros Manseng. Thick skins and loose bunches protect against rot, and it is often used for late-harvest sweet wines (passerillé by desiccation rather than botrytized). It has high acidity and a flavor spectrum of stone fruits. Top wines may be monovarietal, but blends with some Gros Manseng are common.
Courbu	More formally *Petit Courbu* (there is also a related variety called *Courbu Blanc*). Has faintly honeyed citrus character. It is included as a small part in blends of dry or sweet white wines in several appellations, most notably in Pacherenc du Vic Bilh.
Camaralet	An old variety, but now almost extinct due to the difficulty of growing it, it has a strongly flavored profile of citrus and exotic fruits with spicy notes. What is left is mostly used in blending.
Arrufiac	Aromatic variety with a few plantings left in Pacherenc du Vic Bilh.

Jurançon without any qualifier is always sweet. More recently, Jurançon Sec has been introduced as a category for dry white wine, and has been increasing in importance; currently it's about a third of all production. The grape varieties are the same as for the sweet wine. Usually the Sec is vinified in stainless steel, while the Jurançon is matured in old barriques. Independent producers represent about a third of production; the rest goes through the coop.

Vineyards are planted on hillsides facing south to southeast, which shelters them from the wind. The typical altitude is 300-400m. Vines may run up the slope, but when the slopes are steep, it is more common to find terraces, often arranged in an amphitheater. The southern part of the appellation has terroirs of clay and sandstone. The northwestern part has lighter terroir of sandstone. The northeastern part has the terroir known as the poudingues (pudding stones) of Jurançon; these are sedimentary rocks covered in calcareous pebbles and siliceous gravel. In this area, Chapelle la Rousse (near Pau) is considered to be one of the most expressive terroirs in the appellation, giving lively wines that age well.

The terraced vineyards at the Jardins des Babylone are typical of Jurançon.

Style in Jurançon is determined by date of harvest, with grapes for dry wines usually harvested around September, grapes for the moelleux in October-November, and grapes for some super-concentrated Vendange Tardive cuvées as late as December. Some exceptional dry wines are harvested at the same time as the moelleux, in order to get a riper fruit spectrum, and they tend to have rather high alcohol, becoming quite spicy and spirity. The sweet wines tend to show apricot fruits and stewed apples, sometimes with a perfumed edge. As the sweet wines move to later harvest they become more concentrated in aroma and flavor, but do not usually seem particularly sweeter. They tend to develop aromas of truffles after about three years, providing a savory counterpoise to the piquant sweet fruits.

A major climatic influence in making it possible to harvest right up to the of the year for the Vendange Tardive, or even into the next year, is the Foehn, the wind that comes from Spain from October on. As a warm morning breeze, it encourage passerillage, the desiccation in the berries that concentrates the juice within.

The terrain in Jurançon is spectacular. Driving around, you find yourself going up and down hills, across the tops of valleys on one track roads, and periodically you see vineyards, usually on steep slopes, sometimes ingeniously terraced. There isn't much sense of an exclusive focus on viticulture, as fields of other crops appear in the valleys. "Visitors to

Grapes for making Jurançon are left on the vine into late autumn or winter and become desiccated by passerillage. Courtesy Domaine Cauhapé.

Jurançon say they don't understand, they can't see vines: that's because suitable locations for vineyards are restricted by the lie of the land," explains Pierre Coulomb at Domaine Guirardel. "Most of the properties are very small, and polyculture is common."

To the west of Jurançon, nestled up to the mountains at the border with Spain, Irouléguy was famous in the Middle Ages for the Abbey of Roncevaux, which was an important stop for pilgrims, and had 1,000 ha of vineyards at its peak. When the AOP was created in 1970, there were only about 50 ha left, and most of the grapes went to the cooperative. Today a handful of artisan growers have resurrected vineyards, which are on steep and rocky slopes. Grape varieties are much the same as the areas to the east, with Cabernets Sauvignon and Franc together with Tannat for reds, and Gros and Petit Manseng together with Courbu for whites.

To the west of Jurançon, nestled up to the mountains at the border with Spain, Irouléguy was famous in the Middle Ages for the Abbey of Roncevaux, which was an important stop for pilgrims, and had 1,000 ha of vineyards at its peak. When the AOP was created in 1970, there were only about 50 ha left, and most of the grapes went to the cooperative. Today a handful of artisan growers have resurrected vineyards, which are on steep and rocky slopes. Grape varieties are much the same as the areas to the east, with Cabernets Sauvignon and Franc together with Tannat for reds, and Gros and Petit Manseng together with Courbu for whites.

Reference Wines for the Pyrenees	
Madiran	Château Montus
Jurançon Sec	Domaine Cauhapé
Jurançon	Domaine Guirardel
Irouléguy	Herri Mina

The Southwest as a whole—both Bordeaux Satellites and Pyrenees—offers a distinctive difference from the rest of France, with neither the edginess coming from marginal climates, nor the full force ripeness of the south. Whether strong reds or sweet whites, the wines tend to be powerful and characterful.

Vintages

From Bergerac to Gaillac, vintages generally follow Bordeaux. The Pyrenees are closer to Languedoc than to Bordeaux; vintages are later here, so good weather in the Autumn can be relatively more important. Given the breadth of the region, and the variety of climatic influences, any guide can only be rather general.

		Dry Wines
2019	*	Not as many problems with extremely dry conditions as the rest of France.
2018	*	Some problems from cool wet Spring, followed by heat reducing acidity in Bergerac, but better conditions in Madiran. More variable in Southwest than rest of France.
2017	*	Frost reduced yields to record lows, but dry wines are good.
2016	*	Best results for reds in Cahors and dry whites in Jurançon.
2015	**	An attractive vintage for reds from Cahors to Gaillac to Madiran. Dry whites are more variable.
2014	*	Difficult conditions all over France, you might even call this the year of the rain. Dry wines variable, sometimes with difficulties reaching maturity.
2013	*	A decent year with a cool start and warm end. Better in the Pyrenees than the Dordogne, where some wines are a bit green.
2012		An average year, with best reds in Gaillac and best dry and whites in Jurançon.
2011		An average vintage, with reds better than dry whites, which suffered from loss of acidity.
2010	**	Best reds in Bergerac, best dry whites in Jurançon, wines can be austere.
2009	***	A very good year here as elsewhere in France, with solid reds from Cahors to Gaillac to Madiran. Dry whites less aromatic than usual.

2008	*	Best reds in Cahors and Madiran, best whites in Jurançon. Acidity can be strong.
2007	*	Relatively cool year with lighter wines.
2006		Dry wines now past their best.
2005	***	A very good year everywhere.

		Sweet Wines
2016	**	Best sweet wines are supple, but overall results are variable.
2015	*	Sweet wines best in Monbazillac, Bergerac, and Saussignac, elsewhere more heterogeneous.
2014	*	Sweet wines more successful than dry, but on the lighter side.
2013	*	Good results in Monbazillac, more variable in Jurançon, wines can be a little austere.
2012		Best results in Jurançon, but few late harvest wines.
2011	**	A rich vintage from Bergerac to Jurançon, but wines can be a little heavy.
2010	***	A great success everywhere.
2009	***	A very good year here as elsewhere in France.
2008		Decent semi-sweet wines, but few great dessert wines.
2007	**	Generally successful, but small volumes.
2006	**	Sweet wines were the success this year.
2005	***	A very good year everywhere.

Visiting the Region

The center of Bergerac is full of narrow medieval streets.

The Southwest is really more a series of separate areas than a single coherent region. Visits need to be organized separately for each area. On the edge of the Dordogne, Bergerac is a lovely old town, with a medieval center, close to the vineyards of

Château Monbazillac is a major tourist attraction and a wine estate owned by the cooperative.

Cahors is the local center for the Lot valley. The famous medieval bridge is a major tourist attraction.

Bergerac AOP and Monbazillac. There are many grand château in the area, including the Château Monbazillac and, farther south, the Château de Duras. It's sometimes possible to combine a visit to a historical chateau with a visit to the wine cellars.

Sixty miles southeast, Cahors is a peninsula, all but surrounded by a U-turn in the river Lot. The whole area is as famous for its production of black truffles as for wine. Farther south you come to Gaillac. Just east of Gaillac, Albi is a major tourist attraction, with its brick-built cathedral.

Moving to the Pyrenees, Pau is a major center for pilgrims, and is just south of the vineyards of Madiran and very close to Jurançon to its south.

Bergerac is quite well organized for tourists, but otherwise, the southwest is not a natural area for oenotourism; some producers maintain tasting rooms, but in general it is best to call ahead for an appointment to be sure someone will be available.

In some appellations, the Syndicat representing the producers has opened a boutique, where wines can be tasted, and purchased at the same price as at the domain. The boutiques are often more accessible— usually in a town center—and have more extended opening hours than the producers themselves (often including weekends). But remember that the lunch break is sacrosanct in France, so most tasting rooms are closed between 12:00 and 2 p.m. They make it possible to directly compare many wines (although the top producers are not necessarily represented); usually tasting is free. They include:

- Les Vignerons de Buzet
  Avenue des Côtes de Buzet, 47160 Buzet-Sur-Baïse
  (+33 5 53 84 17 16) magasin@vignerons-buzet.fr
  www.nouslesvigneronsdebuzet.fr

- Maison des Vins de Bergerac
  1, rue des Récollets, 24100 Bergerac
  (+33 5 53 63 57 55) anis.ward@vins-bergeracduras.fr
  www.vins-bergeracduras.fr

- La Maison des Vins de Fronton
  Château de Capdeville, 31620 Fronton
  (+33 5 61 82 46 33) fronton@france-sudouest.com
  www.vins-de-fronton.com

- Maison des Vins de Monbazillac
  Mairie - LeBourg, 24240 Monbazillac
  (+33 5 53 58 63 13) mtv.mbz@orange.fr
  maisondesvins-monbazillac.jimdofree.com

- Cahors Malbec Lounge
  Place François Mitterrand, Cahors
  (+33 5 65 23 82 35) contact@vindecahors.fr
  vindecahors.fr

- Maison des Vins de Gaillac
  Abbaye St Michel, 81600 Gaillac
  (+33 5 63 57 15 40) vins.gaillac@wanadoo.fr
  www.vins-gaillac.com

- Maison des Vins de Madiran
  L'église, 4 Rue de l'Église, 65700 Madiran
  (+33 5 62 31 90 67) contact@madiran-pacherenc.com
  www.madiran-pacherenc.com

- Maison des Vins du Jurançon
  64360 Lacommande
  (+33 5 59 82 70 30) contactcoeurdebearn.com
  www.vigneronsdujurancon.fr

The etiquette of tasting assumes you will spit. A producer will be surprised if you drink the wine. Usually a tasting room or cellar is equipped with spittoons, but ask if you do not see one (crachoir in French).

Profiles of Leading Estates

Ratings

***	Excellent producers defining the very best of the appellation
**	Top producers whose wines typify the appellation
*	Very good producers making wines of character that rarely disappoint

Symbols

Address

Phone

Owner/winemaker/contact

Email

Website

Principal AOP or IGP

Red   White   Sweet   Reference wines

Grower-producer

Negociant (or purchases grapes)

Cooperative

Conventional viticulture

Sustainable viticulture

Organic

Biodynamic

ha=estate vineyards

bottles=annual production

Tasting room with especially warm welcome

Tastings/visits possible

By appointment only

No visits

Sales directly at producer

No direct sales

Winery with restaurant

Winery with accommodation

24

Dordogne

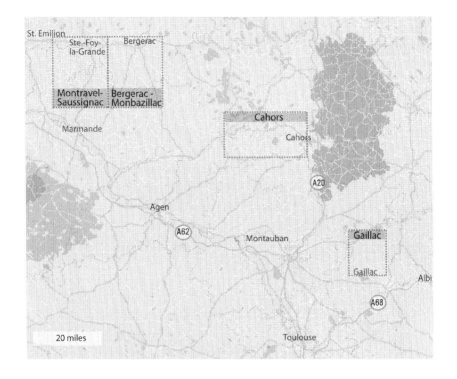

Bergerac

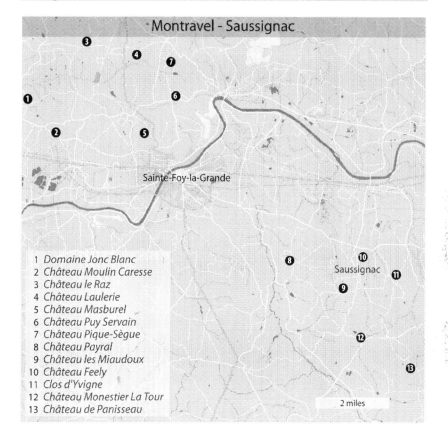

Montravel - Saussignac

Sainte-Foy-la-Grande

Saussignac

1 Domaine Jonc Blanc
2 Château Moulin Caresse
3 Château le Raz
4 Château Laulerie
5 Château Masburel
6 Château Puy Servain
7 Château Pique-Sègue
8 Château Payral
9 Château les Miaudoux
10 Château Feely
11 Clos d'Yvigne
12 Château Monestier La Tour
13 Château de Panisseau

2 miles

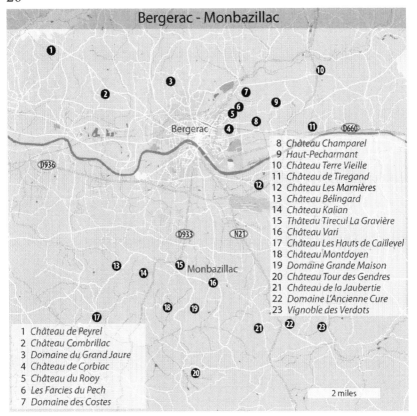

Bergerac - Monbazillac

8 Château Champarel
9 Haut-Pecharmant
10 Château Terre Vieille
11 Château de Tiregand
12 Château Les Marnières
13 Château Bélingard
14 Château Kalian
15 Thâteau Tirecul La Gravière
16 Château Vari
17 Château Les Hauts de Caillevel
18 Château Montdoyen
19 Domaine Grande Maison
20 Château Tour des Gendres
21 Château de la Jaubertie
22 Domaine L'Ancienne Cure
23 Vignoble des Verdots

1 Château de Peyrel
2 Château Combrillac
3 Domaine du Grand Jaure
4 Château de Corbiac
5 Château du Rooy
6 Les Farcies du Pech
7 Domaine des Costes

2 miles

Domaine L'Ancienne Cure

N21, 24560 Colombiers

📞 +33 5 53 58 27 90

Christian Roche

@ contact@domaine-anciennecure.fr

🌐 www.domaine-anciennecure.fr

⬤ Bergerac

Bergerac Sec, l'Abbaye

Monbazillac, l'Abbaye

😊 🏭 🍇 🍷 🖐

50 ha; 180,000 bottles [map p. 26]

From the village at the top of the hill, you get a panoramic view of the domain. Its vineyards extend all the way from the winery at the top, which takes its name from the thirteenth century church in the village, to a tasting room geared for tourists passing along the main road at the bottom. The stone and metal winery building seems somewhat dilapidated outside, but it's all modern equipment inside, with stainless steel tanks for fermentation, and barriques for élevage of the more powerful wines.

The domain was founded by Christian Roche's grandfather when he started to bottle his own wine, although production continued to be split between the estate and the cooperative. The domain owes its present position to Christian, who is clearly a mover and shaker. "We were too limited by size, it was necessary to expand the domain," he says.

The emphasis is on whites, which are three quarters of plantings. There are 3 red cuvées, 3 dry white cuvées, 3 Monbazillac, and 1 rosé and 1 moelleux. They are divided into three brand lines: Jour de Fruit (introductory line); L'Abbaye (mid range); and L'Extase (top of the line). Everything is AOP, Bergerac Rouge or Sec for the dry red or white, Côtes de Bergerac for moelleux, and Monbazillac for fully sweet. There is also a negociant line of wines from Pécharmant. Christian is a late picker, but the style is quite delicate for the dry whites, and verges on savory for the sweet whites; the reds are a little heavier.

Château Tirecul La Gravière ★★

🔲 *24240 Monbazillac*

📞 *+33 5 47 77 07 60*

🔲 *Bruno Bilancini*

@ *contact@tirecul-la-graviere.fr*

🌐 *www.tirecul-la-graviere.fr*

🔲 *Monbazillac*

🕯 *Monbazillac*

😊 🏭 🍇 🖐

8 ha; 12,000 bottles

[map p. 26]

There isn't much doubt that Château Tirecul La Gravière is the best producer in Monbazillac. In the nineteenth century, it was one of 17 grand crus, but production collapsed after phylloxera, and when the AOC was created in 1936, the system of grand crus was not perpetuated. Located on a hill with the Dordogne only a couple of miles away, the site gets botrytis reliably in the mornings, and then the fog blows off in the afternoons. When Bruno Bilancini came here in 1992, grapes were being merged with another property, so he recreated the name of Tirecul La Gravière.

Bruno uses only Sémillon and Muscadelle. "When we arrived here there was a small amount of Sauvignon Blanc. The problem is that its maturity is very different from the others." Sémillon and Muscadelle are complementary. "Muscadelle is almost the opposite of Sémillon in terms of structure. While Sémillon brings richness, creaminess and honey notes, Muscadelle brings balance and freshness to wines containing noble rot, and a complex nose that mixes dried fruits and spices."

Production is almost entirely Monbazillac, divided between Les Pins (from young vines, which means less than 25 years here), the Château wine (vines aged up to 80 years), and Cuvée Madame (selected berry by berry, made only in exceptional years). A Bergerac Sec (dry white) called Andréa du Château Tirecul La Gravière is made in some years from plots that did not get botrytis.

Bruno's policy goes to extremes: the Monbazillac comes exclusively from 100% botrytized grapes, the Bergerac Sec (if any) comes from zero botrytis. These are distinctive wines, very much their own style, spicy in hot years, more herbal in cooler years. "Tirecul needs to wait 8-10 years to develop complexity. It depends less and less on sugar as it ages, and becomes more elegant," Bruno says.

The range was extended considerably in 2016 by buying 6 ha of vines at Saint Perdoux in Bergerac, planted with 70% Merlot, 20% Cabernet Franc, and 10% Cabernet Sauvignon. I haven't tasted the red yet, but I would expect to see the same commitment to quality as in the dry and sweet whites.

Château Tour des Gendres ★

 Les Gendres, 24240 Ribagnac

 +33 5 53 57 12 43

Luc De Conti

@ *familledeconti@wanadoo.fr*

 *www.chateautourdesgendres.com*

Bergerac

Bergerac Sec, Moulin des Dames

53 ha; 250,000 bottles

[map p. 26]

Luc de Conti bought this domain in 1981 with the intention of having a horse farm. The horses are long since gone, but his cousin Francis and son Guillaume are now involved in the domain. The first vintage was 1986, and the domain has been organic since 1996, with a parcel of 12 ha treated as biodynamic. Production was expanded by adding a negociant activity in 2000.

Plantings are Bordeaux varieties, 60% black (Cabernet Sauvignon, Malbec, and Merlot), and 40% white (Sémillon, Sauvignon Blanc, and Muscadelle). The reds are Bergerac or Côtes de Bergerac (for the higher-level cuvées), and the whites are Bergerac Sec, with about 10 cuvées altogether. There are both blends and varietal wines.

Among the whites are a classic Bordeaux blend of all three white varieties (Cuvée des Conti), a varietal Sauvignon Blanc (Moulin des Dames), and an unusual 100% Muscadelle (Conti-ne Périgourdine). The Anthologia cuvée is a varietal Sauvignon Blanc produced only in exceptional vintages (six times in the past three decades). The general style is for gently rounded wines.

Vignoble des Verdots *

Les Verdots, 24560 Conne-de-Labarde

📞 +33 5 53 58 34 31

David Fourtout

@ verdots@wanadoo.fr

🌐 www.verdots.com

Bergerac

Côtes de Bergerac, Chateau Les Tours de Verdots

Bergerac Sec, Grand Vin les Verdots

45 ha; 250,000 bottles

[map p. 26]

The whirlwind that is David Fourtout came into the domain in 1992 when there were only 10 ha of vineyards, but lots of cows. Expanding, David invested in better vinification, aiming for more precision. "It's easy to get tannins and structure here, and I wanted to work my tanks in order to get softer tannins," he says, showing off stainless steel tanks that imitate wood tronconique cuves, made by an old school friend in the next town. Angles vary so that tanks are used according to the desired degree of extraction.

A large new winery was built in 2003 to replace the old cuverie in the village. Below the tasting room is an underground barrel room, which David Fourtout excavated himself, with raw rock exposed at the ends, and a well in the middle revealing the Verdot River below. David is an enthusiast for the latest equipment—fantastic is his favorite description.

With mostly red wine, the estate is exclusively AOP, largely Bergerac and Côtes de Bergerac. Clos de Verdots is the historic range from the 1970s. David started the barrique-aged Château Les Tours de Verdot in 1992, and Grand Vin de Verdot (matured in new oak) in 1995. The top of the line is Le Vin (made only some years). "We try to have a distinct style in each range," he says. Styles extend from forward and fruity to strong structure. There's a common tendency to power, but fruits for the reds become more supple and complex, with intensity increasing along the hierarchy. Whites are relatively savory, with nutty overtones.

Cahors

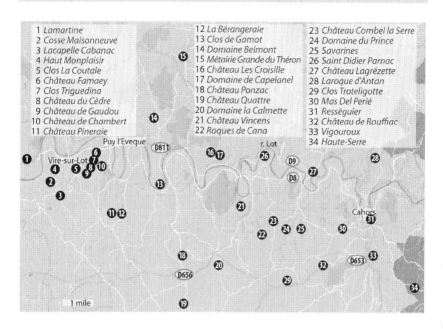

1 Lamartine
2 Cosse Maisonneuve
3 Lacapelle Cabanac
4 Haut Monplaisir
5 Clos La Coutale
6 Château Famaey
7 Clos Triguedina
8 Château du Cèdre
9 Château de Gaudou
10 Château de Chambert
11 Château Pineraie

12 La Bérangeraie
13 Clos de Gamot
14 Domaine Belmont
15 Métairie Grande du Théron
16 Château Les Croisille
17 Domaine de Capelanel
18 Château Ponzac
19 Château Quattre
20 Domaine la Calmette
21 Château Vincens
22 Roques de Cana

23 Château Combel la Serre
24 Domaine du Prince
25 Savarines
26 Saint Didier Parnac
27 Château Lagrézette
28 Laroque d'Antan
29 Clos Troteligotte
30 Mas Del Perié
31 Rességuier
32 Château de Rouffiac
33 Vigouroux
34 Haute-Serre

Château du Cèdre ★★

🔘 *Bru, 46700 Vire-sur-Lot*

📞 *+33 5 65 36 53 87*

👤 *Pascal Verhaeghe*

@

contact@chateauducedre.com

🌐

www.chateauducedre.com

🔘 *Cahors*

🍾 *Cahors, Le Cèdre*

😊 🏭 🍇 🍂

29 ha; 120,000 bottles
[map p. 31]

The Verhaeghe family came from Belgium as refugees during the first world war; Pascal's grandfather was an agricultural worker who married a local girl, and their son took the domain into viticulture. At first he sold wine to negociants, then when Cahors became an AOC, he began to bottle his own wines. Pascal and his brother Jean-Marc took over from their father in 1993. The Cahors vineyards are 90% Malbec, with 5% each of Merlot and Tannat. In addition, there are a couple of hectares with white grapes. There is also a small negociant business, dating from 1995 when they lost the whole crop to hail, and had to buy grapes. There are three cuvées of Cahors and two IGPs under the Cèdre label. Produced from young vines, Château du Cèdre is the only cuvée that is not 100% Malbec. Le Cèdre and the Vieilles Vignes GC come from the same areas, but there are differences in vine age and the proportions of foudres, barriques, and new oak used in élevage. All cuvées are based on blends between vineyards in the third (Mindel) terrace and the calcareous Tran area. "I wanted to make cuvées from each terrace, but we decided there is more complexity in making an assemblage," Pascal says. The general style becomes more refined as you go up the hierarchy, with a big step up from château wine to Le Cèdre, and then GC shows left bank-like style needing time to resolve, with the difference from Le Cèdre more in texture than flavor; it reaches a peak after about fifteen years.

Domaine Cosse Maisonneuve

*

📍 *Les Beraudies, 46700 Lacapelle-Cabanac*

📞 *+33 5 65 24 22 37*

👤 *Catherine Maison-
neuve*

@

*cossemaisonneuve@orange
.fr*

🔴 *Cahors*

🍷 *Cahors, Les Laquets*

📋 🏭 🍇 🥂

30 ha; 130,000 bottles
[map p. 31]

LES LAQUETS

CAHORS
APPELLATION CAHORS CONTRÔLÉE

Cosse et Maisonneuve **2010**
à Lacapelle-Cabanac (Lot)

Coming from north of Paris because she had always wanted to work on the land, Catherine Maisonneuve created the estate with her partner Mathieu Cosse in 1990. Very isolated and completely surrounded by woods, the domain is at the end of a valley, occupying a sort of amphitheater with vineyards all around, rising up to the surrounding woods. Wine is made in a utilitarian warehouse. Different cuvées are made from the top, middle, and bottom of the slope to display the effects of terroir on Malbec. "It's the noble cépage, it's perfectly adapted to the climate here," Catherine says. The bottom is gravel, the middle is more calcareous, and the top is clay over limestone. Wines from the three cuvées taste increasingly refined going up the slope. The difference is due to the tannins, which become increasingly finer-grained. Le Combal from the bottom (12 months élevage) is chewy and a little hard, Lafage from the middle (16 months élevage) shows more precision, and then Les Laquets from the top (24 months élevage) is fine and precise and almost perfumed. Aside from a small proportion of Le Combal that has élevage in cuve, everything is matured in barrique. From a nearby site with yet more clay and limestone comes La Marguerite, the finest of all. There is some new oak in Les Laquets and 100% in La Marguerite. All the Cahors are 100% Malbec. In addition, there are monovarietal Vin de France cuvées of Merlot, Gamay, and Cabernet Franc.

Château Lagrézette *

 Lieu dit Lagrezette, 46140 Caillac

📞 +33 5 65 20 07 42

Alain Dominique Perrin

@

serviceclient@lagrezette.fr

🌐 www.chateau-lagrezette.com

Cahors

Cahors, Château Lagrézette

90 ha; 350,000 bottles

[map p. 31]

By far the most imposing property in Cahors, with a fifteenth century château at the center, Château Lagrézette has vineyards extending as far as the eye can see around the château, planted with 70% Malbec, 26% Merlot, and 4% Tannat. The wide variety of soils ranges from stony, clay and limestone, to pebbles, sand and silt. Château Lagrézette produces four wines, with Michel Rolland as consulting oenologue. Chevaliers Lagrézette is a light, earlier maturing wine made from young vines, and matured in old barriques, but I find it a little tight and rustic. Château Lagrézette is the domain's premium production each vintage, matured like the prestige cuvées in new barriques, and conveying a rather stern impression. Prestige Dame Honneur is produced only in small quantities in the best vintages. These cuvées all come from blends of Malbec and Merlot, with the proportion of Malbec increasing along the hierarchy. Le Pigeonnier comes from a 2.7 ha parcel of Malbec around the old pigeon loft, located near the château. The top cuvées are rich and chocolaty, but with a tendency to high-toned aromatics. Although this rather splendid large property has a spacious tasting room and is nominally open to visits, it is not very welcoming: when I turned up for my appointment, the tasting room was deserted, and a phone call elicited the response, "You have the wrong sort of appointment and I am going home in ten minutes." Caveat visitor!

Clos Triguedina **

Les Poujols, 46700 Vire-
sur-Lot

+33 5 65 21 30 81

Jean Luc Baldès

contact@jlbaldes.com

www.jlbaldes.com

Cahors

Cahors, Clos
Triguedina

65 ha; 400,000 bottles
[map p. 31]

A family property since 1830, Clos Triguedina has been built up into the most important producer in Cahors: since Jean-Luc Baldès, the eighth generation, took over in 1990, he has expanded the domain from its original 22 ha and introduced several new cuvées. "I have stabilized the size. Our mission is to occupy the pole place," he explains. "There are no negociants in Cahors, so we are obliged to do everything, to work out the techniques for viticulture and vinification and to commercialize," he adds. Just outside the extensive cuverie, Triguedina has the oldest Malbec vines in France, planted by Jean-Luc's grandfather who was a nurseryman. There are vineyards on the second, third, and fourth terraces. Vinification is in stainless steel, with élevage in barriques, except for Le Petit Clos, which is effectively an approachable second wine (80% Malbec), but even so is nicely structured. Clos Triguedina is a 100% Malbec classic blend from all terraces, with a strong but fine character. Trilogie comprises a box of three wines, one from each terrace: Au Coin de Bois (2nd terrace) is the most approachable and New World in character; Les Galets (3rd terrace) is more reserved; and Petits Cailles (4th terrace) is the finest in structure. Probus comes from old vines, and is the Vosne Romanée of Cahors. The New Black Wine is effectively a single vineyard cuvée from a 1.3 ha plot of old vines, and is rich but supple. There's also some white wine (a Chardonnay-Viognier blend and a Chenin Blanc, both under IGP Comté Toloson), rosé, and a sparkling rosé made from Malbec. A new tasting room was built recently to encourage oenotourism.

Gaillac

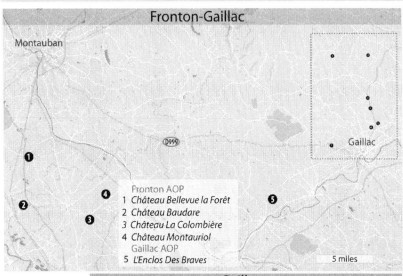

Fronton-Gaillac

Montauban

D999

Gaillac

Fronton AOP
1 Château Bellevue la Forêt
2 Château Baudare
3 Château La Colombière
4 Château Montauriol
Gaillac AOP
5 L'Enclos Des Braves

5 miles

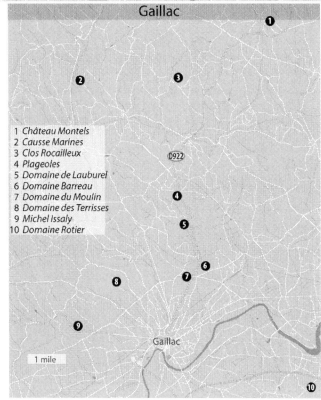

Gaillac

1 Château Montels
2 Causse Marines
3 Clos Rocailleux
4 Plageoles
5 Domaine de Lauburel
6 Domaine Barreau
7 Domaine du Moulin
8 Domaine des Terrisses
9 Michel Issaly
10 Domaine Rotier

D922

Gaillac

1 mile

Domaine de Causse Marines ✱

Le Causse, 81140 Vieux

📞 +33 5 63 33 98 30

Patrice Lescarret & Virginie Maignien

@ contact@causse-marines.com

🌐 www.causse-marines.com

Gaillac

🍷 Vin de France, Causse Toujours

🍷 Vin de France, Zacmau

12 ha; 60,000 bottles
[map p. 36]

Hidden away just outside Vieux, the domain is not particularly well signposted because Patrice Lescarret and Virginie Maignien don't want to be interrupted by cellar door sales. It's very hands-on: Patrice does the grafting himself (he's adamant about not using clones), and when I arrived Virginie was pruning in the vineyard. We had lunch under the trees in a charming garden behind the house, and went through the range of wines, which are now mostly Vin de France. "Since I set up here in 1993 there have been problems with the AOP, and in 2003 and 2004 I stopped using the AOP. Now only the three basic wines are labeled with the appellation, and everything else is labeled as Vin de France," Patrice explains. "Gaillac has special grapes and my objective is to make authentic wine." This is defined as coming from local varieties: whites use Len de l'El, Ondenc and Mauzac; reds use Duras, Braucol, and Prunelard. There is also some Syrah. The dry whites are Les Greilles (a blend in Gaillac AOP), Zacmau (100% Mauzac), and Dencon (100% Ondenc). The reds are Les Peyrouzelles (a Gaillac blend), Rasdu (100% Duras), and Causse Toujours (Syrah and Prunelard). There are several moelleux cuvées, and in exceptional years a fully botrytized cuvée, Folie Pure. The vin de voile is a solera. The style is fresh, with light fruits supported by good acidity, varying between more and less aromatic varieties, but the same intent to avoid heaviness characterizes all the wines.

Michel Issaly

*

817 route de la Ramaye,
Domaine de la Ramaye,
Sainte-Cécile-d'Avès,
81600 Gaillac

+33 5 63 57 06 64

Michel Issaly

info@michelissaly.com

www.michelissaly.com

Gaillac

Gaillac, Le Sang

Gaillac, Quintessence

6 ha; 14,000 bottles
[map p. 36]

Michel Issaly is the sixth generation at this family domain. "We are in the center of the historical part of the Gaillac appellation. I want to make authentic wine," Michel says, defining authenticity as terroir, climate, and preservation of old cépages. The domaine has a single holding running across two valleys, with a friable, very deep limestone base, more calcareous on the top half, more clay on the bottom half, and differences in the microclimates. Average vine age is 40-50 years. "Unfortunately half of my vines are clonal," Michel says unhappily (they were planted by his father). 2013 was his 30th vintage. "I worked for many years conventionally before I had enough experience to work like I do now. I don't like too much temperature control for the reds, I want to respect the vintage. In a hot year fermentation should be hotter. The wine should be a photograph of vintage and cépage," Michel says. "I have pulled my wines out of the appellation because they say they are oxidized. Only two of my cuvées are Gaillac." These are Combe d'Avès (Duras and Braucol) and Le Sang (90% Braucol and 10% Prunelard). Le Grand Tertre reverses the proportions, and another Vin de France, Le Peche de la Tillette, is a blend of four varieties, including a little Merlot. They are fresh, with some herbal impressions. Les Cavaillès is a spicy dry white from Mauzac, Len de l'El, and Ondenc; and Le Vin de l'Oubli is a vin de voile from Mauzac. Quintessence is a sweet white in an oxidative style.

39

Domaine Plageoles

*

Chemin des Très Cantous,
81140 Cahuzac-sur-Vère

📞 +33 5 63 33 90 40

📷 Romain et Florent
Plageoles

@
vinsplageoles@orange.fr

🌐 www.vins-
plageoles.com

🍷 Gaillac

Gaillac, Mauzac

30 ha; 90,000 bottles
[map p. 36]

2009
CÉPAGE MAUZAC VERT

PAR ROBERT & BERNARD PLAGEOLES

«CE N'EST PAS LE VIN QUI ENIVRE,
C'EST L'HOMME QUI S'ENIVRE»
CONFUCIUS (551 - 479 AV J.C.)

The domain originated in 1805 and is now run by Bernard Plageoles, the sixth generation. There's building work everywhere, with a modern tasting room in front of the buildings. The old cellars, under the original family house, are now used for the vin de voile. Behind is a practical warehouse with cement cuves. The domain owes its present reputation to Bernard's father, Robert, who made a huge effort to rescue the old varieties of Gaillac. "We wanted to use the old cépages to avoid the programmed wines," Robert says. The Plageoles believe that you can express the terroir only with single cépages, so all the wines are monovarietals. Altogether there are around fourteen different varietal cuvées. "The only cépage we have that isn't local is Syrah," says Bernard, who took over from his father about ten years ago. Red wines come from Prunelart, Mauzac Noir, and Verdanel, as well as Braucol, Duras, and Syrah. Dry whites come from Ondenc and Mauzac Vert, and sweet wines from Mauzac Roux, Muscadelle, Ondenc, and Loin de l'Oeil. There's also a vin de voile from Mauzac Roux, which is unusually powerful, and would be easy to mistake for Palo Cortado sherry. The white I like best is the dry Mauzac, which seems to offer something of the same impression as Gewürztraminer, in smelling sweet but tasting dry. The reds are light and fresh. The old varieties are no longer allowed in Gaillac AOP, so some of the wines are Vin de France.

Pyrenees

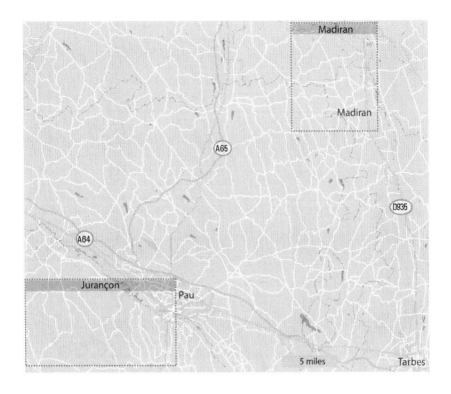

Madiran

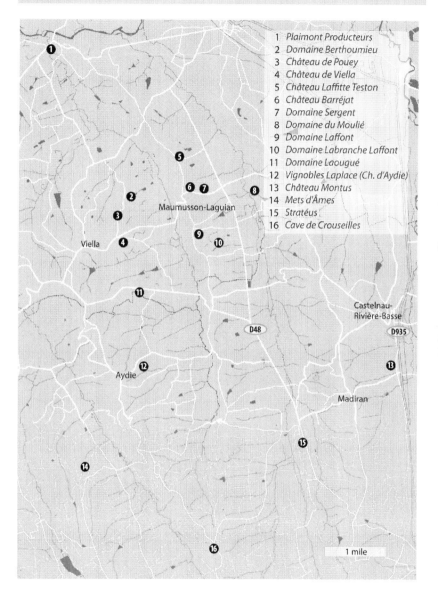

1 Plaimont Producteurs
2 Domaine Berthoumieu
3 Château de Pouey
4 Château de Viella
5 Château Laffitte Teston
6 Château Barréjat
7 Domaine Sergent
8 Domaine du Moulié
9 Domaine Laffont
10 Domaine Labranche Laffont
11 Domaine Laougué
12 Vignobles Laplace (Ch. d'Aydie)
13 Château Montus
14 Mets d'Âmes
15 Stratéus
16 Cave de Crouseilles

Maumusson-Laguian

Viella

Castelnau-
Rivière-Basse

D48

D935

Aydie

Madiran

1 mile

Château Barréjat   *

Barrejat, 32400 Maumusson Laguian

+33 5 62 69 74 92

Denis Capmartin

@

deniscapmartin@laposte.net

www.chateaubarrejat.com

Madiran

Madiran, Seduction

40 ha; 200,000 bottles

[map p. 41]

Denis Capmartin is the sixth generation to run this old family domain, which has some of the oldest vines in France, just near the charming house and terrace. There's a workmanlike winery behind, and viticulture and vinification are modern, focused on bringing out fruit flavors. When phylloxera struck, Denis's great-great grandfather pulled out all the vines, leaving just two small parcels of 4 ha. Up to 200 years old, about 80% Tannat and 20% Cabernet Sauvignon, these pre-phylloxera vines are the basis for the Cuvée de Vieux Ceps (a blend of varieties) and l'Extrême (the best parcel of old Tannat). When Denis took over in 1992 there was only one cuvée of Madiran, but he introduced the vieille vigne cuvées, and divided the major production into two cuvées: Tradition and Seduction are exactly the same blend of 60% Tannat with 40% Cabernet Sauvignon or Franc, but are matured differently, Tradition in cuve and Seduction (introduced in 1996) in barriques. The wines are powerful, in the typical style of the appellation and varieties, but Denis has really mastered the tannins. Tradition still shows a little of the old style Tannat, but Seduction has nicely rounded fruits; and the cuvées from the old, pre-phylloxera vines, really are special in their concentration. There are also dry and sweet white wines under the Pacherenc AOP, and Chardonnay, Cabernet Franc, and rosé under the IGP Côtes de Gascogne, not to mention an Armagnac.

Vignobles Laplace

 Château d'Aydie, 64330 Aydie

📞 *+33 5 59 04 08 00*

 François Laplace

@ *pro@famillelaplace.com*

🌐

www.famillelaplace.com

 Madiran

 *Madiran, L'Origin*

Pacherenc de Vic-Bilh, Château d'Aydie

😊 🏭 🍇 🍷 🚜

58 ha; 6,000,000 bottles
[map p. 41]

François Laplace's grandfather established the domain in 1962, when the Madiran appellation had all but disappeared. Initially confined to the area around the house, vineyards today are located in three different parts of Madiran. "We believe it's always more interesting to make an assemblage. Yes, a terroir is a terroir, but in a warm year St. Lanne will do better, in a wet year Aydie and Moncaup will make the best wine," François says. Madiran is only a third of total production, as most is IGP, made from purchased grapes in a new building full of large stainless steel tanks. There are three cuvées of Madiran, all from estate grapes. The wines are all labeled Famille Laplace. Matured mostly in cuve, the classic cuvée, L'Origine, is Tannat with 30% Cabernet Franc. "When I say classic it's not necessarily a wine of terroir. It's vinification to have simple fruits, not tannin, with a fresh equilibrium. It's true this doesn't have the old typicity of Madiran, but for today's consumer this is a good accompaniment to a meal," says François. "We are looking for Tannat with fruits not tannins." The other two cuvées comes from the slopes of all three locations and are 100% Tannat. Odé d'Aydie is matured in a mixture of foudres and cuves. Château d'Aydie is used as the name for the top wine, and is matured in barriques and foudres. Tight when young, Odé and Château d'Aydie become elegant with age. There are also dry and sweet white wines under the Pacherenc de Vic-Bilh appellation. Since 2005 the team at Château d'Aydie have also been making the wines at Patrick Ducournau's domains, Chapelle Lenclos and Mouréou.

44

Château Montus

★★

32400 Maumusson
  Laguian

📞 +33 5 62 69 74 67

Alain Brumont

@ contact@brumont.fr

🌐 www.brumont.fr

Madiran

Madiran, Cuvée Prestige

☺ 🏭 🍇 ⬤

220 ha; 800,000 bottles
[map p. 41]

By far the largest producer in Madiran, Alain Brumont owns Château Bouscassé (a family property which he took over in 1979 and expanded), Château Montus (founded in 1980), Torus (a blend from young vines of Bouscassé and Montus together with a cooperative), and other domains in Vignobles Brumont. Almost 15 km apart, Bouscassé and Montus are virtually at opposite ends of the appellation. Before Alain bought Montus, it was a farm; he planted the vineyards, and the first wine was made in 1985. The focus is on Tannat. "Tannat made the great Bordeaux, I was very aware of it. I could see that we have very original terroir. I had a chance; because no one was interested in the terroir, I was able to buy vineyards," Alain says. Across the courtyard from the château, a huge new vinification facility has been built into the hillside in three storeys. Underground is a vast barrel room; above is a facility packed with stainless steel tanks, which Alain calls the Church of Tannat. Torus is soft and approachable, Bouscassé has more structure and depth (especially the Vieilles Vignes cuvée), and Montus is full force, with four intense cuvées. Château Montus itself is a blend of Tannat and Cabernet Sauvignon, with 12 months in barrique; Cuvée Prestige is 100% Tannat with up to 24 months élevage; XL is extended for 30 months; and La Tyre is a single-vineyard wine from the best plot, given 18 months élevage. All require years to develop. There are also dry and sweet whites.

Jurançon

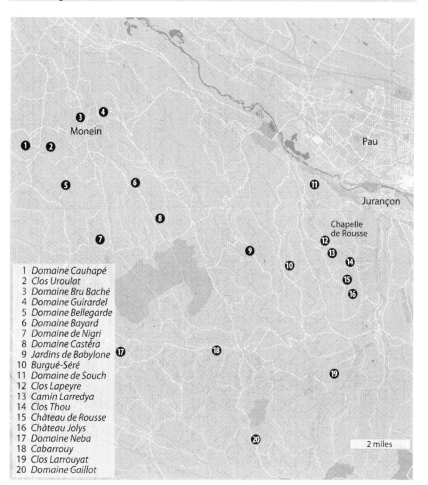

Monein

Pau

Jurançon

Chapelle
de Rousse

1 Domaine Cauhapé
2 Clos Uroulat
3 Domaine Bru Baché
4 Domaine Guirardel
5 Domaine Bellegarde
6 Domaine Bayard
7 Domaine de Nigri
8 Domaine Castéra
9 Jardins de Babylone
10 Burgué-Séré
11 Domaine de Souch
12 Clos Lapeyre
13 Camin Larredya
14 Clos Thou
15 Château de Rousse
16 Château Jolys
17 Domaine Neba
18 Cabarrouy
19 Clos Larrouyat
20 Domaine Gaillot

2 miles

Camin Larredya ★★★

Chapelle de Rousse, 64110 Jurançon

📞 +33 5 59 21 74 42

Jean-Marc Grussaute

@

contact@caminlarredya.fr

🌐 www.caminlarredya.fr

Jurançon

11.5 ha; 45,000 bottles

[map p. 45]

This very old domain is considered to be one of the references of the appellation. More than 800 years old, Camin is local dialect for a chemin (road), and the name Larredya means a place where roof shingles were made from chestnut. Viticulture came later, and in the nineteenth century the domain produced wine for local consumption, until phylloxera arrived. The first Jean Grussaute bought the property in 1900 and grew various fruits. Production of grapes really resumed after 1970, when Jean and Jany Grussaute began to replant the terraces. Some of the vines date from then. Estate bottling started in 1975. Jean's son Jean-Marc, took over in 1988, and withdrew completely from the cooperative. He says that he works the soil like a peasant, and looks after the vines like a gardener.

Located in Chapelle de Rousse, one of the most prestigious parts of the appellation, the property is at an elevation of 300m, reached by a steep, narrow road. Vineyards surround the winery on three side (with forest to the north). Two thirds of production is dry and one third is sweet, each coming from separate vineyards. To the east, both Mansengs and Petit Courbu are grown for the Jurançon Sec. To the west, Petit and Gros Manseng are grown for harvesting later in October and November for the sweet Jurançon. Wines are aged in a mix of barriques and foudres. Each is named for the vineyard where it originates. The first dry wine in the range is La Part Davant, 50% Gros Manseng, 35% Petit Manseng, and 15% Petit Courbu. Aged a little longer, and a little richer, La Virada is 40% Gros Manseng, 20% Petit Manseng, 20% Petit Courbu, and 20% Camaralet. L'Iranja is an orange wine, labeled as Vin de France. The sweet Jurançon is Au Capcèu and is 100% Petit Manseng. There is also a simpler Jurançon, which comes from grapes purchased from the neighboring vineyards, called Costat Darrèr.

Domaine Cauhapé

*

Quartier Castet, 64360
Monein

+33 5 59 21 33 02

Henri Ramonteu

contact@cauhape.com

www.jurancon-
cauhape.com

Jurançon

Jurançon Sec, Seve
d'Automne

Jurançon, Symphonie
de Novembre

43 ha; 260,000 bottles
[map p. 45]

Henri Ramonteu created this domain in 1980, and it is now the largest independent property in Jurançon. "I started with 1 ha, I had to pull it up and replant because the vineyard had been used just to make wine for family consumption," Henri recollects. The estate is an example of the polyculture that's common in the region, with more than 50 ha of corn (and other crops); vineyards extend up to 22 km from the winery. A modern facility has several buildings packed with stainless steel tanks. Sweet wines are matured in barrique. The domain used to produce red wine (as Béarn AOP), but now is exclusively white. "Initially I had to master moelleux, in 1982 I started a sec cuvée. I achieved a certain success because of the aromatic style, then I slowly developed new cuvées," Henri says. Dry wine is as important as sweet here, with style determined by harvest date. Chant des Vignes and Geyser are harvested early; harvested in mid October, Seve d'Automne has more depth of flavor and texture. La Canopée (100% Petit Manseng) is harvested in November at the same time as the moelleux, and has something of the flavor spectrum of the sweet wines. The sweet wines have names reflecting harvest dates: Ballet d'Octobre, Symphonie de Novembre, and then Noblesse du Temps and Quintessence, followed by Folie de Janvier (the last three are 100% Petit Manseng, and only made in some years). The top cuvées here don't increase in sweetness, but show greater complexity.

Domaine Guirardel   *

⊙ *Chemin Bartouille, 64360 Monein*

📞 *+33 5 59 21 31 48*

📇 *Françoise Casaubieilh & Pierre Coulomb*

@ *vin@guirardel.fr*

🌐 *www.guirardel.fr*

🍷 *Jurançon*

🍾 *Jurançon, Bi de Prat*

📅 🏭 🍇 🏺

5 ha; 13,000 bottles

[map p. 45]

Located at the end of a one track road, the domain has vineyards in a single block running down a very steep slope into the valley, planted with 4 ha Petit Manseng and 1 ha Gros Manseng, and then 1 ha of Gros Manseng on the other side. The estate has been in Françoise's family for 400 years; the tasting room is the original house, which was used for vinification for the past 200 years. The centuries' old buildings are packed with modern equipment, and have even been converted to gravity feed by cutting a hole to allow the press to stand on a higher floor above the vats on the ground floor. Françoise and Pierre took over in 2008, increasing plantings, and adding new cuvées. Pierre, who has a questioning eye, has been experimenting to get fresher wines, and dry wines with a spectrum more like the sweet. Pierre describes the Jurançon Sec as a "moelleux without sugar. You can see it's not a typical dry wine, it's the same color as the moelleux," he says. Tradiciou is the cuvée that goes back to Françoise's father. Bi de Casau has been made since 2008 by selecting barrels of Gros Manseng with the most freshness. "We want a half dry effect in the wine, which isn't allowed in Jurançon, but this is our false half dry wine," says Pierre. Bi de Prat, Marrote, and Confit de Manseng are 100% Petit Manseng and come from the end of the vineyard, with Confit picked last. The style tends to be quite spicy. A new project in 2014 was a cuvée called Manseng Nature, where no sulfite is used. Running a small domain, especially with worldwide decline in interest in sweet wines, is difficult, and in 2020 Françoise and Pierre sold to the Perrodo family, who own several châteaux on the left bank of Bordeaux.

Les Jardins de Babylone *

Chemin de Cassioula, 64290 Aubertin

📞 *+33 3 86 39 15 62*

Louis-Benjamin Dagueneau

@ *silex@wanadoo.fr*

Jurançon

Jurançon

3 ha; 6,000 bottles

[map p. 45]

The heart of this tiny estate is a spectacular 2 ha terraced vineyard of Petit Manseng. Didier Dagueneau (famous for his Pouilly Fumé) bought the property, close to Pau, in 2002, in order to make dessert wine, and called it the Jardins de Babylone for its perpendicular appearance. "The Petit Manseng was already planted, but there was nothing here but the vines, as all the grapes had been sold to the coop," says manager Guy Pautrat. The winery was constructed as a group of small buildings just opposite. Didier decided also to make a dry wine, so he planted another hectare nearby with the old lost varieties, Camaralet, Lauzac, and Petit Courbu. Where did he find them, I asked Charlotte Dagueneau? "Papa 'liberated' them from a nursery of old cépages," she explains. Production is split more or less equally between sweet and dry wine, with one cuvée of each. The first vintage was 2002, but it was spoiled by problems with corks, and the first commercial release was 2004. The style here brings the same intensity to bear, whether dry or sweet, that characterizes the Dagueneau wines in Pouilly Fumé. The flavorful dry wine ranges from perfumed to savory depending on the vintage. The sweet wine is matured in a variety of barrel sizes, including French 300 liter and 600 liter, and Austrian 600 liter, each with its own character, as barrel samples show. Once bottled, piquant apricots show lots of concentration on the palate, with impressions of truffles increasing as the wine ages.

Clos Lapeyre   *

257 chemin du Couday, La Chapelle de Rousse, 64110 Jurançon

📞 *+33 5 59 21 50 80*

Jean Bernard Larrieu

@ *contact@jurancon-lapeyre.fr*

🌐 *www.jurancon-lapeyre.fr*

Jurançon

Jurançon, La Magendia

🚶 🍇 🍇 🍇

18 ha; 60,000 bottles

[map p. 45]

Clos Lapeyre is tucked away up a long access road in the foothills of the Pyrenees; it feels quite isolated and much higher than it really is, as you are surrounded by peaks, but it's only 400 m elevation. Originating as a domain with traditional polyculture, it has focused exclusively on viticulture since 1985, when Jean-Bernard Larrieu, grandson of the founder, constructed the first vinification facility. The tasting room is in a charming old house, but just behind is a modern winery, on the edge of a very steep vineyard that Jean-Bernard was busy replanting when I arrived. Vineyards are in many separate parcels, increased about 50% in 2004 by purchase of the nearby Nays-Labassère domain. There are three dry wines and four sweet wines, divided into three ranges. Lapeyre has one dry and one sweet cuvée, and is matured in cuve to emphasize fruit. More complex, La Magendia and Vitage Vielh each spend 1 year in barrique. Then there are the cuvées exceptionelle, either dry or sweet depending on the year. The cuvées are based on varying proportions of Gros and Petit Manseng. The sweet wines come from late harvest of grapes with passerillage, but for the cuvée exceptionelle Vent Balaguer, this is augmented by drying the berries further in the sun. "It's very, very concentrated, almost like a digestif." The dry wines are slightly perfumed, with something of the impression of apricots that characterizes the sweet wines. The sweet wines can be quite herbal, showing truffles as they age.

Domaine de Souch   *

 Chemin de Souch, 64110 Laroin

📞 *null*

 Jean René & Yvonne Hegoburu

@ *domaine.desouch@neuf.fr*

🌐 *www.domainedesouch.com*

 Jurançon

🍾 *Jurançon Sec*

👤🏭🍇🍷

6 ha; 20,000 bottles

[map p. 45]

This small domain started as a retirement project when Yvonne and René Hegoburu purchased a ruined house on the top of a hill just across the river from Pau for their retirement. The property has about 20 ha, half of which are woods. The plan was to plant a vineyard, but René died before this could be accomplished. Although Yvonne had been involved in administration at Château de Viaud in Pomerol, she had not made wine, but in 1987 she planted a small vineyard, running down the slope from 325 m elevation. Vines had been grown on the site in the seventeenth century by Jean de Souch, for whom the domain is named, but had perished with phylloxera. Known today as one of the grand characters of the region, Yvonne now runs the domain together with her son Jean-René. Plantings are 70% Petit Manseng, 20% Gros Manseng, and 10% Courbu. The blend of the Jurançon Sec follows the vineyard plantings, while the Jurançon has equal proportions of Petit and Gros Manseng. Both are matured in stainless steel. The Jurançon cuvée Marie Kattelin (named after Yvonne's granddaughter) is 100% Petit Manseng, and is directly pressed from partially de-stemmed grapes into barriques. It's been described as a "monster of concentration," and is usually one of the richest wines of the appellation. From time to time there are other cuvées, including Pour René, matured in 100% new barriques. The rich sweet wines classically show notes of truffles as they develop.

Domaine Herri Mina   *

64220 Ispoure

+33 5 57 74 59 80

Jean-Claude Berrouet

@
berrouet@jpmoueix.com

Irouléguy

2 ha; 8,000 bottles

About 20 miles to the southwest of Biaritz, Irouléguy is deep into the Basque country, very close to the Spanish border. Its most famous winemaker is Jean-Claude Berrouet, a native of the region who was the winemaker at Petrus for four decades, but has been making wine in Irouléguy since his retirement since 2007 at a small domain he purchased some years previously. He calls his estate Herri Mina from the Basque terms herri (meaning country) and mina (meaning homesick). Vineyards are on steep slopes of the Pyrenees facing south. The white wine is a blend from Gros Manseng (more than half), Petit Corbu, and Petit Manseng (about 5%); it has a distinctive character mingling elements of sweet, savory, and spicy. The red is Cabernet Franc, fermented in stainless steel and aged in old barriques.

Mini-Profiles of Important Estates

Bergerac

Château Bélingard

24240 Pomport
+33 5 53 58 28 03
Laurent de Bosredon
contact@belingard.com
www.belingard.com

80 ha; 200,000 bottles
[map p. 26]

Bélingard means 'sun garden' in Celtic, and claims to be on a site used by the Druids in the fifth century BCE. In an elevated location, today it offers a splendid view across the vineyards. It has been a family estate since 1820, and Laurent de Bosredon is the seventh generation. Vineyards have calcareous-clay soils on slopes ranging from 130m to 200m. The major part of the vineyards is 50 ha in Pomport, of which 28 ha are in AOP Monbazillac. There are another 30 ha in Monestier in AOP Bergerac. As vineyards are being replanted, the vine density is being increased. The entry-level range has red, rosé, dry white, and semi-sec under AOP Bergerac. There is also a zero-sulfite cuvée of Bergerac red. The Reserve range has Bergerac red (50% Cabernet Sauvignon, 50% Merlot, aged in barriques including some new oak) and white (85% Sauvignon Blanc, 15% Sémillon, with some wood exposure), and Monbazillac (70% Sémillon with some botrytis, aged in barriques). The top dry wines are the Lyvress Bergerac (100% Sauvignon Blanc harvested late, aged for 18 months in barriques) and the Côtes de Bergerac Ortus red (65% Merlot, 15% Cabernet Sauvignon, and 20% Malbec, aged in barriques with 30% new oak for 18 months). In Monbazillac there are two heavily botrytized cuvées, Ortus (from successive passes through the vineyard) and Blanche de Bosredon (100% botrytized berries selected individually).

Château Bellevue-la-Forêt

5580 Avenue de Grisolles, 31620
Fronton
+33 5 34 27 91 91
Philippe Grant
cblf@chateaubellevuelaforet.com
www.chateaubellevuelaforet.com

104 ha; 300,000 bottles
[map p. 36]

Consisting of the largest single block of vineyards in Southwest France, the domain has been owned since 2008 by Philippe Grant from England. There's a wide range of reds and rosés, all dominated by Negrette (Fronton must have more than 50% Negrette) with other varieties being Syrah, Cabernet Sauvignon and Cabernet Franc. Micro-oxygenation after fermentation is used to soften the tannins. Classique Rouge is a blend with 55% Negrette, while Mavro is 100% Negrette, both aged in cuve. Forêt Royale is a blend aged in 1-year and 2-year barriques, and Optimum comes from a single plot and ages in barriques with a third new oak. La Forêt rosé is 85% Negrette. Under IGP Comté Tolosan, there are two whites, a Viognier varietal, and a Roussanne-Petit Manseng blend.

Château Champarel

1637 Chemin du Hameau de
Pecharmant, 24100 Bergerac
+33 5 53 57 34 76
Françoise Bouché
champarel@wanadoo.fr
chateau-champarel.fr

6.7 ha [map p. 26]

Located at the top of Pécharmant hill, this small domain is housed in a series of buildings dating from the thirteenth century. It has been owned by the Bouché family since 1971. Vineyards face south on the slope with soils of calcareous clay on a base of limestone. Plantings are 55% Merlot, 25% Cabernet Sauvignon, and 20% Cabernet Franc. The regular cuvée ages for 12-16 months in barriques; the Prestige cuvée ages for 18 months with 30% new barriques. The domain produces only red wine under the Pécharmant AOP.

54

Clos d'Yvigne

Bourg, 24240 Gageac et Rouillac
+33 5 53 22 94 40
contact@vigneronsdesigoules.fr
www.vigneronsdesigoules.com

21 ha
[map p. 25]

This domain became famous as the result of a book and TV program describing Patricia Atkinson's experience in becoming a winemaker after she moved from Britain to the Dordogne. Starting with 4 ha, she learned viticulture and winemaking and built the domain into a successful project producing Bergerac Sec (white), Côtes de Bergerac (red),and Saussignac (sweet). The wines achieved critical acclaim. Patricia still owns the vineyard, but in 2014 she sold the brand to the local coop (Les Vignerons de Sigoulès), which now makes the wines.

Château Combrillac

Impasse de Coucombre, 24130 Prigonrieux
+33 5 53 23 32 49
Florent Girou
contact@combrillac.fr
www.combrillac.fr

15 ha
[map p. 26]

Florent Girou took over his family estate in 2008. Vineyards are in a single block, close to the town of Bergerac, with 7 ha of black varieties and 8 ha of white varieties. Thre is a full range of Bergerac, white from Sauvignon Blanc with Sémillon, rose from Cabernet Sauvignon, and red from Merlot with a little Cabernet Sauvignon. In addition to the regular range, Florent produces the Les Inédits cuvées — intended to showcase terroir — with the white from a single parcel of Sauvignon Blanc, and red from 90% Cabernet Sauvignon. Le Dôme comes from a plot of Cabernet Sauvignon high up the slope and fermtnts and then ages in 500-liter barrels. There is also a sweet wine from Rosette.

Château de Corbiac

Route de Corbiac, 24100 Bergerac
+33 5 53 57 20 75
Antoine de Corbiac
corbiac@corbiac.com
www.corbiac.com

20 ha; 80,000 bottles
[map p. 26]

Emphasizing a distant family connection to (the real) Cyrano de Bergerac, the winery dog is called Cyrano. This was a considerable estate in the seventeenth century, with 260 ha of farms and vineyards. The Huguenot-style château sits quite grandly in a park of 120 ha. The family has been here since the sixteenth century, and is now in the seventeenth generation in the form of Antoine de Corbiac, who recently joined his mother Thérèse. The flagship wine is Pécharmant, dominated by Merlot. Visitors report widely varying experiences, from those who were delighted by being given old vintages to taste, to those found the reception brusque and unwelcome.

Domaine des Costes

4, rue Jean-Brun, 24100 Bergerac
+33 5 53 57 64 49
Jean-Marc Dournel
contact@domainedescostes.fr
www.domainedescostes.fr

11 ha; 45,000 bottles
[map p. 26]

This old domain was rented out until oenologue Jean-Marc Dournel and his wife Nicole took it back in 1992. Jean-Marc consults for several properties in Bergerac including Domaine de l'Ancienne Cure (see profile), Château Tour des Gendres (see profile), and Vignoble des Verdots (see profile). The winery, which was renovated in 1999, is in Bergerac; the vineyards are in Pécharmant, divided more or less equally between Cabernet Sauvignon, Cabernet Franc, and Merlot. Cuvée Tradition is the flagship wine from Pécharmant; Grande Réserve was introduced in 1998 as a selection from the best plots. Both age in barriques, with one third new for Tradition and 100% new for Grande Réserve. The rosé comes from Cabernet Franc.

Château Les Farcies du Pech

Les Farcies du Pèch, 24100 Bergerac
+33 6 75 28 01 90
Serge & Betty Dubard
sbdubard@gmail.com
www.farciesdupech.com

15 ha; 80,000 bottles [map p. 26]

The Dubard family moved to the region in the 1970s, when they established Château Laulerie (see mini-profile). Vignobles Dubard extended its holdings when Serge and Betty acquired Château Les Farcies du Pech in Pécharmant in 2000. They restructured the vineyards and renovated the winery. Soils are sand and gravel over a layer of iron-rich clay known locally as 'tran'. The estate wine is a blend of a quarter each of Cabernet Sauvignon, Merlot, Cabernet Franc, and Malbec, aged in oak with a third each of new, one-year, and two-year barriques. Elixir is a special cuvée of Malbec with a production of only 5,000 bottles.

Château Feely

Lieu Dit La Garrigue, 24240
Saussignac
+33 5 53 22 72 71
Caro Feely
caro@chateaufeely.com
www.feelywines.com

9 ha
[map p. 25]

Château Feely is really into oenotourism. Caro and Sean Feely started their career in wine in South Africa, but moved to France where they bought Château Haut Garrigue in Saussignac. Renamed as Château Feely, the property now produces wines under the Vin de France label (identified as Terroir Feely because the use of 'château' is restricted to AOP wines). In reds, La Source is 80% Merlot and 20% Cabernet Sauvignon, while Grace is an equal blend of the varieties, and Vérité is 100% Cabernet Sauvignon. In whites, Sincérité is 100% Sauvignon Blanc, Silex is 100% Sémillon, and Générosité is 90% Sémillon with 10% Sauvignon Blanc. Committed to biodynamic viticulture, wine production is only one of the activities at Château Feely, which offers an extensive series of visits and tastings, and wine tours. The wines are not only organic, but vegan too.

Domaine du Grand Jaure

16 Chemin de Jaure, 24100 Lembras
+33 5 53 57 35 65
Bertrand & Bernadette Baudry
domaine.du.grand.jaure@wanadoo.fr
www.domainedugrandjaure.com

16 ha
[map p. 26]

Brother and sister Bertrand and Bernadette Baudry are the fourth generation at this family domain, which was purchased by their great grandfather in 1920 with only 4 ha. Their father established the domain in its present form when he planted black varieties for making Pécharmant, and started estate bottling in 1970. Bernadette et Bertrand took over in 1992 and in 2000 extended production into sweet wine from Rosette. Black varieties are planted on iron-rich clay, and whites on sandy-pebbly soils. The Pécharmant cuvées are blends of Merlot, Cabernet Franc, and Cabernet Sauvignon. Cuvée Tradition ages in vat; Cuvée Terroir ages in used barriques; and Cuvée Mémoire is a selection of the best lots, aged in new barriques. The white Bergerac Sec ages in barriques. The Rosette has the first grapes to be harvested and is light and sweet.

Domaine Grande Maison

Lieu-dit La Grande Maison, 24240
Monbazillac
+33 5 53 58 26 17
Benjamin Chabrol
contact@grandemaison-
monbazillac.com
www.grandemaison-
monbazillac.com

14 ha; 80,000 bottles [map p. 26]]

The 'grande maison' is a fortified manor house, dating back to the fourteenth century. The property was acquired in 1990 by Thierry Després, who re-planted virtually all of the vineyards, and was a pioneer of organic viticulture in the region. In 2012, Jean-Louis Cabrol and his son Benjamin bought the property. It's a very hands-on operation: Benjamin, who is the winemaker, conducts tours and visits. Vineyards face full south, and there's a small artifi-cial lake that moderates climatic conditions and helps to provide mist to sponsor botrytis. There's a range of dry wines in Bergerac AOP; red and rosé are 100% Merlot, white is 80% Sauvignon Blanc, aged in cuve. The top dry wines are variously called Cuvée La Tour or Tête de Cuvée, with the red under Côtes de Bergerac (90% Merlot); they age in new barriques. The focus of the domain is on Monbazillac, where there are four cuvées. The basic Cuvée des Anges has 80% Sémillon, 10% Sauvignon Blanc, and 10% Muscadelle and is lightly botrytized. With more botrytis, aged in cuve to keep freshness, Cuvée Exotique is all Sauvignon, 60% Sauvignon Blanc and 40% Sauvignon Gris. More conventional, Cuvée du Château comes from 60-year-old vines of 60% Sémil-lon, 20% Sauvignon Blanc, and 20% Muscadelle, heavily botrytized, and ferments and ages in new barriques for 30 months. Cuvée des Monstres comes from 70-year-old vines of 60% Sémillon, 30% Muscadelle, and 10% Sauvignon; deeper in color, it ferments and ages in new barriques for 36 months.

Château Grinou

Route de Gageac, 24240 Monestier
+33 5 53 58 46 63
Catherine & Guy Cuisset
chateaugrinou@aol.com
www.chateau-grinou.com

30 ha; 140,000 bottles [map p. 25]

The vineyards of Château Grinour are all around the village of Monestier, with the winery consisting of a converted barn. Guy and Catherine have spent the last three decades making wine here, and now their sons Gabriel and Julien have taken over. Part of a new approach is to abandon the restrictions of the AOP Bergerac and label the wines as IGP Périgord or Vin de France. The change starts in the vineyards. where the Guyot pruning method required by the AOP has been replaced by a 'hedge,' which the brothers feel gives better quality by generating more but smaller berries. In the entry-level range, Cuvée Tradition is 70% Merlot and 30% Cabernet, while the white is half each of Sauvignon Blanc and Sémillon. A new range at the same price point is called Les Petites Perdrix, and has a Merlot and a Sémillon-Sauvignon blend. The reserve range has a 100% Merlot and a 100% Sauvignon Blanc. The top wines are also monovarietals, 100% Merlot for the Grand Vin, and 100% Sémillon for the sweet Saussignac.

Domaine du Haut-Pécharmant

Peyrelevade, 24100 Bergerac
+33 5 53 57 29 50
Didier Roches
contact@haut-pecharmant.fr
www.haut-pecharmant.fr

35 ha [map p. 26]

Didier Roches is the fifth generation at this family estate on the top of the Pécharmant hill, and is pres-ently President of the growers' association. The winery was constructed in 1978 when the family left the cooperative and started estate-bottling. Vine-yards fall into parts: Clos Peyrelevade was the first vineyard in the estate, in 1915, consisting of 10 ha on sandy-gravelly soil, just across the road in AOP Rosette; while the heart of today's domain is 25 ha on blue clay based on the layer of rocks locally called 'tran' in Pécharmant. They are bottled sepa-rately, under the names respectively of Clos Peyrelevade and Haut-Pécharmant. Corre-sponding to the terroirs, Clos Peyrelevade is forward and fruity, while Haut-Pécharmant is more serious. From Clos Peyrelevade there are red and rosé under IGP Périgord, a red Pécharmant, and a sweet Rosette. The estate wine from Haut-Pécharmant is dominated by Cabernet Sauvignon and Cabernet Franc, with some Merlot and Malbec. Cuvée Veuve Roches comes from older vines. The top wine is Cuvée Prestige, which aged in barriques.

Château de la Jaubertie

24560 Colombier
+33 5 53 58 32 11
Maïté Doffin
mdoffin@chateau-jaubertie.com
www.chateau-jaubertie.com

50 ha; 200,000 bottles [map p. 26]

After Nick Ryman sold the Rymans chain of stationers in Britain in 1971, he purchased Château Jaubertie, and poured money into the property in an attempt to make high quality wine in Bergerac. Originally surrounded by 27 ha of vineyards, the château dates from the sixteenth century and was a hunting house for Henri IV. There were financial difficulties in the eighties, and in 1991 Nick Ryman sold the property to his son, Hugh, who was in the English wine trade. Vineyards cover three terroirs: very thin soil on rocks at the top, calcareous in the middle, and clay at the bottom. There are more or less equal black and white varieties of the region, although the white includes 3 ha of Chardonnay. The range starts with Cuvée Tradition, including a Merlot-based red (aged in new American oak), a Sauvignon-based white (aged in sued barriques), and rosé (a blend of Merlot and Cabernet Sauvignon). The Vieilles Vignes red Bergerac is 80% Merlot and 20% Cabernet Sauvignon, and the moelleux Bergerac (sweet but not botrytized) is 100% Muscadelle. The top wines are the Cuvée Mirabelle range, selected from the best parcels. The red is 45% each of Merlot and Cabernet Sauvignon, with 10% Cabernet Franc, and ages in new oak; the white Bergerac is a classic blend of 80% Sauvignon Blanc and 20% Sémillon, barrel fermented and aged in oak. There is also a Cuvée Mirabelle Monbazillac, made from a block that develops botrytis; it's 65% Sémillon and ages in 50% new barriques.

Domaine Jonc Blanc

24230 Vélines
+33 5 53 74 18 97
Isabelle Carles & Franck Pascal
jonc.blanc@free.fr
joncblanc.fr

17 ha; 80,000 bottles [map p. 25]

Jonc Blanc is named for the local terroir, a white limestone plateau with very thin soils that results in low yields. Isabelle Carles and Franck Pascal left Paris to start the winery in 2000. Franck also makes Champagne near Reims. The focus is on natural winemaking: no addition of sulfur, no fining, no filtration. This led to a clash with the AOP. "It is regrettable that the development of a wine respectful of life and natural processes that allow its development, often results in an incompatibility with the tasting criteria imposed by the AOC," Franck says, so he left the Bergerac AOP in 2012, and now most of the wines are Vins de France. The reds are blends of Cabernet Sauvignon, Merlot, and Malbec. Cuvée Fruit is aged in cuve and foudres to bring out the fruit, while Racine ages in barriques. Both spend extended time, 18-24 months, on the lees. Whites may be labeled variously as Bergerac Sec, Côtes de Montravel, or Côtes de Bergerac, depending on sweetness level. Fleur is a blend of Sauvignon Blanc, Sauvignon Gris, and Sémillon, aged in stainless steel, and Ecorce (originally called Acacia) is 100% Sauvignon Blanc from old vines harvested very late, then fermented and aged in 400-liter barrels. The Pure range consists of monovarietals made from single plots, and includes Merlot, Malbec, Sémillon, and Gros Manseng. The domain describes itself as "Authentic and 'natural' wines—with or without AOC."

Château Kalian

Bernasse, 24240 Monbazillac
+33 5 53 24 98 34
Kilian Griaud
kalian.griaud@wanadoo.fr
www.chateaukalian.com

10 ha
[map p. 26]

Anne and Alain Griaud purchased the property with only 5 ha in 1992, and their son Kilian took over in 2007, armed with a degree in oenology from the University of Dijon, and experience at Clos Haut-Peyraguey in Sauternes. Most of the plantings are Sémillon; 90% of production is sweet white wine. From Monbazillac there are four cuvées: the Monbazillac is aged in barriques, the SGN is highly botrytized and ages longer, and there are varietal wines from Muscadelle and Sauvignon. The dry wines are all Bergerac; the red ages in barriques, but the cuvée Juste à Temps has no added sulfur and ages in steel.

Château Laulerie

Le Gouyat, 24610 Saint-Méard-de-Gurçon

+33 5 53 82 48 31

Grégory & Marine Dubard

contact@vignoblesdubard.com

www.vignoblesdubard.fr

85 ha; 600,000 bottles

[map p. 25]

Part of the Domaine du Gouyat, the largest domain in the appellation, which the Dubard family established in 1977, Château Laulerie produces a range of wines under the Bergerac and Montravel appellations and IGP Périgord. In addition to blends of red, white, and rosé in Bergerac AOP, there are varietal wines of Merlot, Malbec, and Cabernet Franc. Juste Terre is a Cabernet Franc that ages in amphora, and Juste Ciel is a 100% Sémillon. Comtesse de Ségur is used for the wines from Montravel: the red is 80% Merlot and 20% Malbec; the white is 100% Sauvignon Blanc. The wines are labeled as Bergerac in the United States. Vignobles Dubard also owns châteaux in Lalande de Pomerol and Puisseguin St. Emilion.

Château les Marnières

La Conne, 24100 Bergerac

+33 5 53 58 31 65

Christophe Geneste

chateaulesmarnieres@orange.fr

www.chateaulesmarnieres.com

32 ha; 120,000 bottles

[map p. 26]

This family estate is in the hands of the sixth generation under Reine and Christophe Geneste. Mostly in Bergerac, with a couple of hectares in Pécharmant, plantings are 60 black varieties and 40% white. There are some old vines here, with an average age for blacks of 30 years, and for whites about 60 years. Bergerac red is 60% Merlot and ages in cuve, while Côtes de Bergerac is 80% Merlot and ages in barriques. The higher-end reds are Pécharmant, with Les Pierres Levées being the general blend, and the top wine, Le Sillon Rouge, coming from a parcel acquired in 2010, aging in barriques for 16 months. There's a range of whites from Bergerac. In dry wines, l'Eglantier, is 60% Sémillon, aged in barriques; La Côte Fleurie comes from the best plots and includes 70-year-old Muscadelle, aged in new barriques for 18 months. There's also Côtes de Bergerac (moelleux) and Monbazillac.

Château Masburel

Fougueyrolles, 33220 Sainte Foy La Grande

+33 5 53 24 77 73

Chris Walker

chris.walker@chateau-masburel.com

www.chateau-masburel.com

22 ha; 70,000 bottles

[map p. 25]

The property dates from 1740 and was owned by members of the Royal Court until the Revolution. Its modern history dates from 1997 when it was purchased by Olivia and Neil Donnan, who restored the château and installed a modern winery, The Donnans retired from active management in 2008, and in 2018 sold the property to Chris Walker and Irma Lazickiene from Britain, who are once again restoring vineyards and renovating the winery. The property is located in Montravel, and the focus has been on reds, with Cabernet Sauvignon and Merlot representing three quarters of plantings. The top wines are the Bolero cuvée of Montravel red and the Cotes de Montravel sweet white. The reds from the Côtes de Bergerac are predominantly Merlot with a small proportion of Cabernet Sauvignon.

Château les Miaudoux

Les Miaudoux, 24240 Saussignac
+33 5 53 27 92 31
Gérard Cuisset
contact@chateaulesmiaudoux.com
chateaulesmiaudoux.com

29 ha; 170,000 bottles
[map p. 25]

Gérard et Nathalie Cuisset bought this property, which is located in the small sweet wine appellation of Saussignac, in 1987. Vineyards are planted with about two thirds white varieties and are mostly in the Bergerac AOP. There are two sweet wine cuvées: Côtes de Bergerac moelleux, and Saussignac, which comes from the oldest vines and is 60% Sémillon, 40% Muscadelle, aged in new barriques. Dry wines start with Bergerac Sec or Bergerac Rouge, which are aged in cuve. Next come Cuvée Elaïa, 100% Merlot aged partly in barriques, with no added sulfur, and Rouge Fût, 80% Merlot and 20% Cabernet Franc, aged in oak. The top of the range are the Inspiration des Miaudoux cuvées, which are among the richer wines of the appellation. The white Bergerac Sec is 100% Sauvignon Gris, fermented and aged in acacia. The red Bergerac is 70% Merlot, 20% Cabernet Franc, and 10% Cabernet Sauvignon, aged in new barriques.

Château Monestier la Tour

Lieu-dit La Tour, 24240 Monestier
+33 5 53 24 18 43
Mathieu Eymard
contact@chateaumonestierlatour.com
www.chateaumonestierlatour.com

30 ha; 100,000 bottles [map p. 25]

The château is quite a grand building, on the site of a thirteenth century fort, surrounded by a 100 ha estate. The property underwent two recent major changes. In 1998, Philip de Haseth-Möller undertook a major renovation. In 2012, he sold the property to Karl-Friedrich Scheufele, owner of the jeweler Chopard and also the Caveaux de Bacchus that distributes Romanée Conti in Switzerland. Production restarted from scratch, with Stéphane Derenoncourt as consulting oenologist. A new winery has been constructed, and a herbarium has been introduced for making biodynamic preparations. Vineyards are on clay-limestone on slopes, with 14 ha of black varieties and 11 ha of white varieties. Black plantings are 67% Merlot, 23% Cabernet Franc, 7% Cabernet Sauvignon, and 3% Malbec, and there are two red cuvées. The Bergerac cuvée, Cadran, is close to half of production, and there is a much smaller amount of Côtes de Bergerac. Wines age in barriques with up to a third new oak. There is also a Bergerac rosé. The Bergerac Sec is the largest production white, coming from Sauvignon Blanc, Sémillon, and Muscadelle. There's a very small production of sweet white under Saussignac AOP in some vintages. Watch for future developments.

Château Montdoyen

Le Puch, 24240 Monbazillac
+33 5 53 58 85 85
Jean-Paul Hembise
contact@chateau-montdoyen.com
www.chateau-montdoyen.com

40 ha; 120,000 bottles [map p. 26]

Formerly called Château Le Puch, the estate had been abandoned when Jean-Paul and Brigitte Hembise bought it in 1996, planted vineyards after taking a geological survey, and resumed wine production under the new name. Their son Gonzague is now involved. Just under half of the 83 ha estate is planted with vines, at the relatively high density of 5,500 /ha, with a little more white than black varieties. Un Point C'est Tout is the entry-level range, and includes Bergerac red, white, and rosé. The equivalent in Monbazillac is Marquis de Montdoyen. Ainsi Soit-Il is the mid-level range, including Bergerac white, Côtes de Bergerac red, and Monbazillac. The top wines have individual names. Divine Miséricorde is Bergerac Sec with 35% Sauvignon Blanc and 65% Sémillon, barrel-fermented and then aged in the barriques for 11 months. It's known for its exotic character. Under Côtes de Bergerac, Ni Oui, Ni Non is 80% Cabernet Franc and 20% Cabernet Sauvignon; Tout Simplement is 55% Merlot and 45% Cabernet Franc; and l'Imparfait is 95% Cabernet

Sauvignon and 5% Merlot. All age in barriques for 14-16 months. The Monbazillac, Femme Je Vous Aime, is 70% Sémillon, 20% Sauvignon Blanc, and 10% Muscadelle, and is barrel-fermented followed by aging in the barriques for 26 months.

Château Moulin Caresse

1235 route de Couin, 24230 Saint Antoine de Breuilh

+33 5 53 27 55 58

Famille Defarge

contact@moulincaresse.com

www.moulincaresse.com

50 ha; 275,000 bottles

[map p. 25]

This family domain has been in the same family since 1749. Sylvie and Jean-François Deffarge have been in charge since 1981, today with their sons Benjamin and Quentin. Vineyards are in Montravel and Bergerac, with two thirds planted to black varieties. The entry-level wines are all monovarietals: the Montravel Sec is Sauvignon Blanc, the Côtes de Montravel Moelleux is Sémillon, and the Bergerac Rouge is Merlot. The slightly higher-level Magie d'Automne range has conventional blends for each appellation. The Cent Pour 100 cuvées come from best plots in Montravel and include dry white, red, and liquoreux. The top red wine is Coeur de Roche, a selection of the best berries, vinified in 400-liter barrels.

Château de Panisseau

24240 Thénac

+33 5 53 58 40 03

Emmnanuel Guiot

contact@panisseau.com

www.chateaudepanisseau.com

50 ha

[map p. 25]

Chateau de Panisseau started as a castle, built by the English during the fourth crusade in the twelfth century. Owned by a series of families, in 1990 it was sold to Groupe Suez (specialists in water management). This is a sizeable property, with the vineyards in an estate of 106 ha. Black grapes are planted on calcareous terroir, white on soils with more clay. The large size of the estate allows production of a wide range of wines. Classique is the entry-level range, including red, white, and rosé from Bergerac. Under Moulin de Panisseau, the red is a Côtes de Bergerac from 50% Cabernet Sauvignon, 44% Merlot, and 6% Malbec, and is aged in barriques; the white is Bergerac Sec, from 56% Sauvignon Blanc with 22% each of Sémillon and Muscadelle, barrel-fermented and aged in oak. Château de Panisseau Rouge is Côtes de Bergerac, a blend of Merlot and Cabernet Sauvignon from the best plots, aged in new barriques. Château de Panisseau Blanc has similar composition to the Moulin white, but is a selection from the best plots.

Château le Payral

Le Bourg, 24240 Razac-de-Saussignac

+33 5 53 22 38 07

Thierry Daulhiac

contact@le-payral.com

www.le-payral.com

15 ha; 80,000 bottles

[map p. 25]

Thierry and Isabelle Daulhiac were the third generation when they took over the family estate in 1992. It's located between the sweet wine appellation of Monbazillac and the eastern outpost of Bordeaux, Sainte-Foy-La-Grande. Plantings include 8 ha of white vines and 7 ha of black vines. Most of the white produces Bergerac Sec, but there's also a small amount of Saussignac (sweet) from Sémillon in years when botrytis occurs. There's also a moelleux (semi-sweet) cuvée called Tutti Frutti. The dry white is half Sauvignon Blanc and about a quarter each of Sémillon and Muscadelle. Cuvée Petite Fugue has 60% Sauvignon Gris and ages in oak. Bergerac is half Merlot and about a quarter each of Cabernet Sauvignon and Cabernet Franc. Lou Payral is 100% Merlot and vinified without adding sulfite. Cuvée Héritage is a Côtes de Bergerac red.

Château de Peyrel

21 Route de Peyrel, 24130
Prigonrieux
+33 6 07 27 59 65
Franck Decourroux
chateau.peyrel@orange.fr
chateaudepeyrel.com

8 ha; 30,000 bottles
[map p. 26]

Franck Decourroux gave up his career in finance to take over this small domain in 2013. Everything had to be started from scratch. In whites, the Bergerac Sec and Rosette are both 80% Sémillon, 15% Muscadelle, and 5% Sauvignon Blanc. They age on the lees in cuve for 12 months. The difference is that Rosette uses only free-run juice. Two whites age in oak for 12 months, the Rosette Cuvée Excellence (70% Sémillon and 30% Muscadelle), and Bergerac Renaissance (97% Sémillon and 3% Muscadelle), named to reflect the revival of a vineyard that had been abandoned in 1950. The Bergerac red is 50% Cabernet Sauvignon and 25% each of Cabernet Franc and Merlot, and ages in tank for 12 months. The domain started with 6.5 ha and in 2016 Franck bought another 1.5 ha with the aim of being able to add a longer-lived red to the range.

Château Pique-Sègue

Mallard, 33220 Port Sainte Foy et
Ponchapt
+33 5 53 58 52 52
Marianne & Philippe Mallard
chateau-pique-segue@wanadoo.fr
chateaupiquesegue.com

60 ha
[map p. 25]

This domain has a split personality. Part of the 200 ha estate is given over to viticulture and part is used for breeding a herd of polled (without horns) Limousin cows. The 30 ha of black grape varieties are mostly planted with 80% Merlot and 20% Cabernet Sauvignon. The 36 ha of whites have Sauvignon Blanc, Sauvignon Gris, Sémillon, and Muscadelle. The domain is one of the largest producers in Montravel. Under AOP Bergerac there are red and rosé; whites are Montravel (dry) or Côtes de Montravel (sweet). The top reds are the Côtes de Bergerac, Château Dauzan La Vergne, 75% Merlot aged for 12 months in barriques, and the Montravel Terre de Pique Sègue, 90% Merlot aged for 15 months in barriques.

Château Puy Servain

Calabre, 33220 Port Sainte Foy et
Ponchapt
+33 5 53 24 77 27
Daniel Hecquet
oenovit.puyservain@wanadoo.fr
www.puyservain.com

49 ha; 300,000 bottles
[map p. 25]

Alfred Hecquet came to the area after the first world war, and then in 1943 bought the property, sending grapes to the cooperative. His son started estate bottling under the name of Château Puy Servain, and today the domain is run by the next generation, oenologue Daniel Hecquet. Puy Servain is used on the label for the top wines, a range of Montravel and Haut Montravel. The focus is on the liquoreux, which include Terrement and Suprême, both botrytized 100% Sémillon. The flagship red is the Montravel Rouge Vieilles Vignes, a blend of 80% Merlot and 20% Cabernet Franc, aged in 60% new oak for 15 months. Wines are also produced under the labels of Château Calabre (Bergerac red, dry white, moelleux, and rosé), Domaine des Bertranoux (Pécharmant), and Haut-Sarthes (Montravel and Bergerac).

62

Château le Raz

Vignoble Barde, 24610 Saint-Méard-de-Gurçon

+33 5 53 82 48 41

Patrick Barde

vignobles-barde@le-raz.com

www.le-raz.com

65 ha; 650,000 bottles

[map p. 25]

The Barde family has been involved in winemaking or related activities for generations, and acquired the Château le Raz in 1958 with 35 ha. Today there are 28 ha of white vines and 32 ha of black. The terroir has calcareous-clay slopes and a plateau of siliceous soil on top of iron-rich subsoil. The Bergerac Classique comes from 20-year old vines and is 75% Merlot, with Cabernet Franc, Cabernet Sauvignon, and Malbec, aged in cuve. The cuvée Grand Chêne comes from 30-year old vines of 90% Merlot with 10% Cabernet Franc, and ages in barriques with one third new oak. Young vines (less than 12-years) are used to produce rosé. The white is 70% Sauvignon Blanc, and ages on the lees in cuve. There are also IGP wines.

Château du Rooy

Rosette, 24100 Bergerac

+33 6 78 75 11 55

Gilles & Laetitia Gérault

contact@chateau-du-rooy.com

www.chateau-du-rooy.com

20 ha; 75,000 bottles

[map p. 26]

When the owners retired in 1998, Gilles Gérault rented the estate, and two years later he purchased the property, including the fourteenth century building. The vineyards weren't in very good condition, and have been continuously restructured since 2003. A new winery was built in 2011 and 2012. Vineyards are divided between Bergerac (both black and white varieties) and Pécharmant (black only). From Bergerac there are cuvées in red, white, and rosé, aged in vat. Rosette de Rooy is a sweet (nonbotrytized) white. The top wines are the Folly du Rooy; the white is Bergerac Sec, the red is Pécharmant. Both age in barriques.

Chateau Terre Vieille

Le Pinié, 36 route de Grateloup, 24520 Saint-Sauveur

+33 5 53 57 35 07

Gérôme & Dolores Morand Montei

contact@terrevieille.com

www.terrevieille.com

13 ha; 60,000 bottles

[map p. 26]

At the heart of the Pécharmant AOP, this old domain had been abandoned after phylloxera, and was resurrected by the Morand Monteil family. Gérôme came from Paris, Dolores was working at a negociant in Bordeaux, and they started the domain in 1989. They have now been joined by their children. Vineyards are divided into 10 plots of Merlot, Cabernet Sauvignon, Cabernet Franc, and a little Malbec. Soils are clay-silex on the iron-rich base of *tran*. The four cuvées are all Pécharmant AOP. Chevalier and Divin are entry-level, the estate wine is 65% Merlot and ages for 16 months in barriques, and the top wine is Ambroisie, also dominated by Merlot, aged for 20 months in barriques.

Château de Tiregand

118, route de Sainte-Alvere, 24100 Creysse

+33 5 53 23 21 08

François-Xavier de Saint-Exupéry

contact@chateau-de-tiregand.com

www.chateau-de-tiregand.com

40.5 ha; 180,000 bottles [map p. 26]

A large domain for Pécharmant, this has been run by François-Xavier de Saint-Exupéry since he returned from his studies in oenology in 1984. Vineyards are only a small part of the 400 ha estate, with a grand château dating back to the thirteenth century and mostly built in the eighteenth century (it's a Historical Monument), and cellars from the seventeenth century. There are tours around the exterior of the château, and the terrace and gardens are open during September and on France Heritage days. Tours of the wine cellars are available every day. The white and rosé are AOP Bergerac; the white is 90% Sauvignon Blanc, aged briefly on the lees before bottling. With only 2 ha devoted to white plantings, this is a small part of production. The reds are all Pécharmant, among the richest and longest-lived of the appellation. The entry-level wine is Clos Montalbanie, 35% each of Merlot and Cabernet Franc, with 20% Cabernet Sauvignon and 10% Malbec, aged in cuve. It's treated very much like a second wine in Bordeaux: part comes from young vines, and part comes from lots declassified from the estate wine. Merlot increases in the estate wine to 54%, with 23% Cabernet Sauvignon, 18% Cabernet Franc, and 5% Malbec. Coming from 20-year-old vines, it ages in oak with 20% one-year barriques. This is the major part of production, with 160,000 bottles. The top wine is Grand Millésime, with grapes sourced from 8 ha on south-facing slopes with soils of iron-rich clay. The blend is 60% Merlot, 35% Cabernet Sauvignon, and 5% Cabernet Franc. It ferments partly in cuve and partly in barriques, and then ages for 18 months in barriques with 50% new oak and 50% one-year oak. Production is about 8,000 bottles.

Château Vari

Lieu dit Pataud, 24240 Monbazillac
+33 5 53 61 84 98
Sylvie & Yann Jestin
contact@chateau-vari.com
www.chateau-vari.com

22 ha; 80,000 bottles [map p. 26]

Sylvie and Yann Jeston bought Château Vari in 1994. Vineyards are on clay and limestone soils with a limestone base, with 14.5 ha in Monbazillac, 5 ha devoted to red, and 0.5 ha of white varieties for dry wine. Red (two thirds Merlot and one third Cabernet Sauvignon), rosé, and dry white are all Bergerac AOP, all aged in cuve. Monbazillac is the heart of the domain, with five cuvées. The blends are the estate wine and the Reserve, both dominated by Sémillon, coming from successive passes through the vineyard, fermented and then aged in barriques for 9-14 months depending on vintage; the Reserve is made only in better years. There are also three cuvées from the individual varieties: Cuvée Sauvignon is more or less at the level of the estate wine, but consists of 100% Sauvignon Blanc; Cuvée Muscadelle comes from the oldest Muscadelle; and the top wine, La Cuvée Gold, comes from 60-year-old Sémillon, harvested berry by berry, then aged in barriques for 24 months.

Côtes de Duras

Château Haut Lavigne

Michau Lavigne, 47120 Astier-de-Duras
+33 5 53 20 01 94
Nadia Lusseau
nadia.lusseau@tele2.fr
www.hautlavigne.com

8.5 ha

Oenologist Nadia Lusseau took over this small domain in 2002. Plantings are half white and half black Bordeaux varieties, on clay and clay-limestone. Cuvée Nadia describes the entry-level line, fermented and aged in concrete, with red and dry white (both Côtes de Duras), and moelleux and rosé (both Vin de France). Cuvée La Miss, subsequently renamed Cuvée G, comes as dry white (60% Sauvignon Blanc, 40% Sémillon) or red (80% Merlot, 15% Cabernet Sauvignon, 5% Malbec), aged in barriques; both are Côtes de Duras. Cuvée Miss-Terre is a selection of best white barriques, with 80% Sauvignon Blanc and 20% Semillon, and ages for 18 months in barriques followed by 18 months in cuve. It is a Vin de France.

64

Domaine Mouthes Le Bihan

Mouthes, 47120 Saint Jean de
Duras
+33 5 53 83 06 98
Jean-Mary Le Bihan
contact@mouthes-le-bihan.com
www.mouthes-le-bihan.com

23 ha; 80,000 bottles

Catherine and Jean-Mary Le Bihan took over this domain in 2000 and they have two quite different sorts of activity. On the one hand, they produce wine, and have added further plots to their vineyards; and they also breed pure-blood Arab horses. Almost three quarters of the vineyards are planted with black varieties. La Pie Colette is the entry-level wine, with white (50% Sauvignon Blanc, 30% Sémillon, 20% Chenin Blanc), red (80% Merlot, 20% Malbec), and rosé (Cabernet Sauvignon). Vieillefont is a mid-level range, 80% Cabernet Sauvignon and 20% Merlot for the red; the white is 50% Sémillon, 30% Sauvignon Blanc, and 20% Muscadelle, and is made in barriques. Les Apprentis is used for the high-end red, which is 85% Merlot and 15% Cabernet Franc. Pérette et Les Noisetiers is the high-end white, a 100% Sémillon. La Lionne et le Désert is a moelleux from Sémillon.

Cahors

Domaine Belmont

Le Gagnoulat, 46250 Goujounac
+33 5 65 36 68 51
Françoise Belmon
contact@domaine-belmont.com
www.domaine-belmont.com

6 ha; 20,000 bottles
[map p. 31]

The domain is located in the hills northeast of Cahors, outside of the AOP and makes wines under the IGP Côtes du Lot. The vineyard was planted on virgin soils in 1993 by architect Christian Belmon, who died in 2010; his widow runs it today, with Stéphane Derenoncourt consulting on winemaking and Claude Bourguignons consulting on the soils. Initially reds were planted, the whites came later. Three red cuvees are 80% of production, based on Syrah and Cabernet Franc. The whites are Chardonnay. Cuvees are divided into Dolmen which comes from clay terroir and Montaigne which comes from calcareous terroir. The best plot of Syrah has Serine taken from Cote Rôtie. The top wine is a blend of 80% Cabernet Franc to 20% Syrah.

Domaine de la Bérangeraie

Coteaux de Cournou, 46700 Grézels
+33 5 65 31 94 59
Maurin Beranger
berangeraie.juline@orange.fr
www.berangeraie.fr

35 ha; 80,000 bottles
[map p. 31]

André and Sylvie Berenger came from Provence to establish their domain in Cahors in 1971. They bought a ruin with no water or electricity, renovated it, and planted vineyards on the Grèzes soil, an iron-rich clay terroir. Their children Maurin and Juline joined the domain. Vineyards are still harvested manually. The wines fall into three groups: Cahors Tradition is aged in vat; Cahors Élevage ages in barriques; and there are also red and rosé under IGP Lot. In the Tradition range, Juline is 90% Malbec and 10% Merlot, while Maurin is 100% Malbec, and Les Quatres Chambrées is a small production of Malbec from old vines. The Elevage range includes three 100% Malbecs: Les Traversets ages in one third new oak, La Nuit des Rossignols comes from old vines and ages in 1-year barriques, and La Gorgée de Mathis Bacchus comes from a plot on the top terrace. RISS is made in small amounts from vines from the original planting, 95% Malbec and 5% Tannat, on volcanic terroir.

Domaine la Calmette

*390 chemin du Colombier, 46090
Trespoux Rassiels*
+33 6 02 09 00 17
Maya Sallée et Nicolas Fernandez
nicolas@domainelacalmette.fr
www.domainelacalmette.fr

7 ha; 25,000 bottles
[map p. 31]

Maya and Nicolas Fernandez decided to create their domain on the calcareous plateau overlooking the valley of Cahors, starting with a single hectare in 2016. About a third of production goes into a Vin de France, the Serpent à Plumes, a blend of 80% Malbec with 20% Merlot, which is aged on the lees in concrete vats. The Cahors Trespotz is a traditional assemblage from different terroirs, 90% Malbec and 10% Merlot, aged in concrete vats. Bois Grand is the top wine, a Cahors blend of 70% Malbec with 30% Merlot coming from a single parcel on the plateau, where the vines are intermingled and the two varieties are picked and fermented together. It ages in 3-4-year old barriques. The wines are neither fined nor filtered, and minimal or even zero sulfur is used.

Domaine de Capelanel

Fages, 46140 Luzech
+33 6 81 62 66 48
Sébastien Dauliac
sebastien.dauliac@orange.fr

14 ha; 30,000 bottles
[map p. 31]

This family domain dates from 1878 and is in its fifth generation under Sébastien Dauliac, who is considered to be one of the new generation making wine up on the heights. The domain's particular feature is that vineyards are on iron-rich (siderolythic) soils, and include 70-year-old Malbec vines (planted by Sébastien's grandfather, who had a nursery). The style has lightened and become less extracted since Sébastien took over in 2002. Titouan has been made since 1998 and is a Malbec aged in vat. Mythique comes from the oldest vines and ages in new oak barriques. Amphût is 100% Malbec and ages in a mixture of amphora and Austrian oak.

Château de Chambert

Les Hauts Coteaux, 46700 Floressas
+33 5 65 31 95 75
Philippe Lejeune
info@chambert.com
www.chateaudechambert.com

58 ha; 150,000 bottles
[map p. 31]

This old domain of Cahors was famous in the nineteenth century (when it had almost 400 ha), and was given new life when it was purchased in 2007 by Philippe Lejeune, who comes from the region and was a successful entrepreneur in IT. No expense has been spared to restore the reputation of the Château, which is now the largest biodynamic property in the area. The Château Chambert cuvée comes from 30-year old vines of 85% Malbec and 15% Merlot. The Grand Vin is 100% Malbec from the oldest vines. Both age in 20% new and 80% 2-year barriques. A second wine called L'Allée de Chambert was introduced at a lower price point in 2011. In addition there is a line of entry-level 'bistro' wines, and a fortified wine called Rogomme.

66

Clos la Coutale

46700 Vire-sur-Lot
+33 5 65 36 51 47
Philippe Bernède
info@coutale.com
closlacoutale.com

90 ha; 400,000 bottles
[map p. 31]

Philippe Bernède is the sixth generation at this family domain, which was established in 1895. The vineyards are in two adjacent parcels, each forming an amphitheater; the higher has glacial terroir, and the lower, on the floor of the valley, is alluvial gravel. Philippe has been refining his style, and today Clos La Coutale has 80% Malbec and 20% Merlot to make it more approachable. Grande Coutale is a super-cuvée, coming from lower yields (only 25 hl/ha) with a composition of 70% Malbec and 15% each of Merlot and Tannat. Clos La Coutale is fermented in stainless steel and aged in a mix of foudres and 1- and 2- year barriques, while Grand Coutale is fermented in foudres and aged in new barriques.

Clos de Gamot

46220 Prayssac
+33 5 65 22 40 26
Martine & Yves Jouffreau-Hermann
contact@famille-jouffreau.com
www.famille-jouffreau.com

25 ha; 60,000 bottles
[map p. 31]

The Jouffreau family has been making wine at the Clos de Gamot for 300 years. The Clos de Gamot is a 15 ha vineyard on the second and third terraces, planted exclusively with Malbec, including some vines planted just after phylloxera in 1885. Clos St. Jean is a 10 ha vineyard on a hill above the village of Sals that was resurrected in 1993 by planting at high density. (In 1971 they bought Château de Cayrou, another property with 30 ha of vineyards, but they sold it in 2009.) Wines are produced separately from each vineyard. Clos de Gamot is 100% Merlot, and there is also a cuvée from the oldest vines, the Cuvée des Vignes Centenaires Le Gamotin is a second wine from the clos, easier to drink than the two more "serious" wines. Clos St. Jean is a blend of Malbec and Merlot. The wines are fermented in concrete vats and aged in 600-liter barrels. There's also a range of entry-level wines under the name of Les Saisons du Lot.

Domaine Rességuier

173 Chemin du Bourg Lacapelle,
46000 Cahors
+33 6 86 61 85 12
Laurent Rességuier
laurent@domaine-resseguier.fr
www.domaine-resseguier.fr

8.5 ha
[map p. 31]

One of the relatively few producers in the vicinity of Cahors itself (only a couple of miles away), this family estate is now run by the fourth generation; Laurent took over in 2000 after completing his studies in oenology. He expanded the estate from an initial 3 ha, and produces three red cuvées from 60% of production, selling the rest to negociants. Les Amandiers comes from young vines, and ages for 18 months in concrete, Lou Travers comes from 30-year-old vines and ages in barriques for 16 months, and Balandrié comes from 40-year-old vines, aging for 16 months in new barriques. There is a rosé under the IGP Côtes du Lot.

Combel la Serre

Lieu-dit Cournou, La Serre, 46140
Saint Vincent Rive d'Olt
+33 5 65 21 04 09
Julien& Sophie Ilbert
contact@combel-la-serre.com
combel-la-serre.com

22 ha; 150,000 bottles
[map p. 31]

Julien Ilbert is one of the new wave producers in Cahors. When started in 1998, the family domain was engaged in polyculture and sent its grapes to the coop. He expanded the vineyards, which are planted almost entirely with Malbec; Julien has avoided the other traditional varieties and has no Merlot. He provided grapes to Cosse Maisonneuve until he started bottling his own wines in 2005. The entry-level wine is Le Pur Fruit du Causes, vinified in cement. The eponymous Château Combel la Serre is aged first in stainless steel and then in wood for a year. This is by far the largest production wine. Le Lac aux Cochons comes from a parcel of 90-year old vines, and ages in 600 liter barrels. Au Cerisier and Les Peyres Levades are also cuvées from single parcels.

Crocus

c/o Maison Georges Vigouroux,
Route de Toulouse, 46003 Cahors
+33 5 65 20 80 82
Bertrand Gabriel Vigouroux & Paul
Hobbs
info@crocuswines.com
www.crocuswines.com

10 ha; 42,000 bottles

A partnership between Maison Georges Vigouroux (see mini-profile) and American winemaker Paul Hobbs, Crocus reflects the trend for New World winemakers to try their hand at Malbec in Cahors. Paul is based in California's Sonoma Valley, but also makes wine in Argentina. His collaboration with Vigouroux started in 2009, and now produces five cuvées, all 100% Malbec. Atelier comes from the third and fourth terraces and ages in stainless steel, Calcifère ages for 18 months in half new and half one-year barriques, La Roche Mère ages in new barriques for 24 months, Prestige represents the traditional approach of blending from different terroirs, and ages for 18 months in half new, half one-year barriques, and Grand Vin is a selection of the best parcels from the third terrace and the plateau, aged for 24 months in new barriques.

Château Les Croisille

46140 Fages, Luzech
+33 5 65 30 53 88
Famille Croisille
chateaulescroisille@wanadoo.fr
www.lescroisille.com

30 ha; 100,000 bottles
[map p. 31]

The domain was created in 1979 when Bernard and Cécile Croisille rented an abandoned property on the Causse (plateau) at Luzech. They cleared land and planted vineyards until the estate reached its present size. At first grapes were sold to the local coop; in 1994 they started to bottle their own wine in space rented from a neighbor, but moved into their own winery in 2000. In 2007 and 2015 their sons Germain and Simon joined the domain. Le Croizillon is a blend of Malbec from several terroirs, Silice is Malbec specifically from iron-rich terroir, and Calciare is Malbec exclusively from calcareous terroir. All age in used barriques. La Pierre has the unusual character of aging in a vat created in limestone. Divin Croisille comes from the best parcels of older vines, and ages in a mix of 500-liter barrels and 30 hl oak casks. Grain par Grain is made by picking single grapes, and vinifying and aging them in 500-liter barrels. There are also white wines from Sauvignon Blanc and Chardonnay. Causse du Vidot is a special cuvée, made in association with Mendoza producer Alto Los Hormigos, and intended to express limestone.

Château de Gaudou

46700 Vire-sur-Lot
+33 5 65 36 52 93
Fabrice Durou
info@chateaudegaudou.com
www.chateaudegaudou.com

60 ha; 300,000 bottles
[map p. 31]

The imposing château is located on the third terrace, in a cluster of important producers including Clos Triguedina and Château du Cèdre. The Durou family has been making wine here for seven generations. Estate bottling started relatively early, in 1966. The style has been modernized, from its former oak-driven character to a more fruit-forward approach, and the range extended by introducing new cuvées. The entry-level cuvée, Tradition, is an assemblage of lots of Malbec, Merlot, and Tannat from all terraces, and ages for 9 months in foudre. Under the description, 'Grand Vins,' there are three cuvées, all from old (30-60-year) vines on the third terrace. Grand Lignée is 85% Malbec and 15% Merlot, aged for 10-15 months in barriques. Renaissance is a parcel-selection of 100% Malbec, and ages for 18 months in barriques. Le Sang de ma Terre was introduced in 2013; also 100% Malbec, it comes from a particularly sunny plot at the top of the third terrace, and ages in concrete eggs for 9 months. Réserve Cailau comes from a 1 ha plot of the oldest (60-year) vines; 100% Malbec, with lower yields than the other cuvées, it ages in a standard (225 liter) barrique and a 600 liter demi-muid. There are also some white wines and rosé and a red IGP Côtes du Lot

Château Famaey

Les Inganel, 46700 Puy l'Évêque
+33 5 65 30 59 42
Maarten & Luc Luyckx
chateau.famaey@wanadoo.fr
www.chateaufamaey.com

40 ha
[map p. 31]

The property actually dates from 1850, but its modern incarnation started when Luc Luyckx and Marc van Antwerpen, originally from Belgium, bought the property in 2001. Luc's son Maarten became the winemaker in 2003. Vineyards extend from the first to the third terraces. Wine from the first terrace is labeled as IGT Côtes du Lot, and the second and third terraces are used for Cahors, all 100% Malbec. The terroir is gravel and clay. The Tradition cuvée ages in stainless steel, while Fût de Chêne ages in barriques. There are also some special cuvées. Cuvée F ages in ovoid tanks, Cuvée S has no added sulfur, and the top Cuvée X comes from the oldest vines. Cuvée X is Sauvignon Blanc, and there is also a series of entry-level wines labeled as Chevaliers Fanaey.

Château Haut Monplaisir

Monplaisir, 46700 Lacapelle
Cabanac
+33 5 65 24 64 78
Cathy Fournié
chateau.hautmonplaisir@wanadoo.fr
chateauhautmonplaisir.com

29 ha; 150,000 bottles
[map p. 31]

Cathy Fournié took over the estate, then only 15 ha, in 1998 from her father, who had sold the grapes to negociants. Cathy and her husband Daniel started estate bottling, helped by brothers Pascal and Jean-Marc Verhaeghe of Château du Cèdre (see profile), who continue to consult. Vineyards are on the third terrace, with soils of clay and pebbles, with 25 ha classified for Cahors, and 4 ha in IGP Côtes du Lot. There are four cuvées under AOP Cahors. The entry-level wine is Tradition, aged 70% in cuve and 30% in wood. Prestige is a step up, with 24 months aging in barriques with one third new oak. L'Envie is a sulfur-free cuvée, from 30-year-old vines, aged for 12 months in 500-liter barrels. The top wine comes from 50-year-old vines: Pur Plaisir ferments in barriques and then ages for 30-36 months in the same barriques. All are 100% Malbec. There's also a white Chardonnay-Viognier blend, and rosés, which are IGP Côtes du Lot.

Château de Haute-Serre

Hauteserre, 46230 Cieurac
+33 5 65 20 80 20
Bertrand-Gabriel Vigouroux
hauteserre@g-vigouroux.fr
hauteserre.fr

60 ha; 360,000 bottles
[map p. 31]

Named for the owners in the Middle Ages, Haute-Serre was a famous estate, producing wine until 1880 when phylloxera killed the vineyards. Georges Vigouroux bought the abandoned estate in 1970, cleared the land and planted Malbec, and built a winery. His son Bertrand-Gabriel now runs the estate as part of Maison Georges Vigouroux (see mini-profile). Vineyards are on the Kimmeridgian terroir of the Plateau Calcaire. Lucter is 100% Malbec aged in cuve, Seigneur is 90% Malbec with 7% Merlot and 3% Tannat, aged in barriques with one third new oak, and Gérone Dadine uses fermentation of 100% Malbec in 400-liter barrels of new oak to make a classic Black Wine. There's also a small production of Chardonnay. At Haute-Serre there is now a Michelin-starred restaurant, and Vignobles Vigouroux also owns the hotel Château de Mercuès (which also produces wines of Cahors), the 36 ha Château Leret Monpezat in Cahors, and Château Tournelles in Buzet.

Château Lacapelle Cabanac

Le Château, 46700 Lacapelle
Cabanac
+33 5 65 36 51 92
Thierry Simon & Philippe Vérax
contact@lacapelle-cabanac.com
www.lacapelle-cabanac.com

19 ha; 80,000 bottles [map p. 31]

Thierry Simon and Philippe Vérax were in software in Paris when they decided on a change of career to winemaking. In 2001, they bought a property that had been converted into wine production in 1978, and renovated it. This is an old site for winemaking, as there are vestiges of a chai from the eighteenth century. Vineyards are in two blocks, one on the Causse (the Kimmeridgian terroir on the plateau), and one on a limestone plateau. There are five cuvées of Cahors. Le Château is the entry-level cuvée, 80% Malbec and 20% Merlot, vinified traditionally, which is to say in concrete for 6 months. Prestige is 90% Malbec and 10% Merlot, and spends 18 months in oak. Malbec XL is 100% varietal, and ages for 20 months in new barriques. Malbec Original is a return to history—"the cuvée that perhaps represents the best expression of our terroir"—coming from a late harvest and aging for 8 months in concrete. Cahors no SO2 is 90% Malbec and 10% Merlot, and has no added sulfur, aging for 9 months in concrete. Under IGP Côtes du Lot, there are several entry-level wines; the red comes from Cabernet Sauvignon, a dry rosé comes from Malbec, and there is also a sweet rosé.

Château Lamartine

Lamartine, 46220 Soturac
+33 5 65 36 54 14
Benjamin & Lise Gayraud
cahorslamartine@orange.fr
www.cahorslamartine.com

37 ha; 220,000 bottles [map p. 31]

During the phylloxera crisis, the Gayraud family built houses, including the property at Lamartine in 1883. By the 1920s they were running a farm, and some plots of vines were planted as part of polyculture. Estate-bottling started in 1955, and the farm focused exclusively on viticulture from 1971. Alain Gayraud's parents inherited the estate, and Alain took over from his grandparents in 1976, when he was only 19. His children Benjamin and Lise took over in 2016. Almost at the western border of the appellation, the microclimate is influenced by the Atlantic. Vineyards face south. Tandem is used to describe the entry-level wines, a white blend of Chardonnay, Viognier, and Chenin Blanc under IGP Côtes du Lot, and a 100% Malbec Cahors with minimal extraction, aged in concrete eggs and tanks for 6 months. Benjamin is also straightforward, 85% Malbec and 15% Merlot, from various terroirs, aged in stainless steel. Cuvée du Tertre and the estate Cahors are more traditional, 90%

Malbec and 10% Merlot, blended from three terraces, aged in a mix of concrete and oak. Cuvée Particulière is more ambitious, coming from 40-60 year-old vines on the second and third terraces, aged in a mix of large oak vats and barriques for 12-14 months. Expression is a parcel selection, from a 5 ha plot of Malbec on the third terrace, aged for 24 months in new barriques. Particulière and Expression require some time to come around.

Domaine Laroque d'Antan

Ancienne Route de Paris, Laroque
des Arcs, 46090 Bellefont-La Rauze
+33 06 30 96 14 17
Emmanuel Bourguignon
domaine@laroquedantan.com
www.laroquedantan.com

6 ha; 4,000 bottles [map p. 31]

Claude Bourguignon is a soil scientist who became known for his view that modern farming methods have destroyed the life of the soil. "In France, I find soils that have less biological activity than the Sahara," he famously said. After thirty years working on terroir, this is the first time he has produced wine. Claude and his wife Lydia found a site a couple of miles north of Cahors, just outside the appellation—"this gives us more freedom to choose grape varieties," Lydia says. The parcel has Kimmeridgian soils that had been abandoned for 140 years. They cleared the slope, keeping the hedges and trees. Their son Emmanuel is in charge of the domain, which they planted with old varieties, all obtained by selection massale from well-known vineyards: 2 ha of Sauvignon Blanc (from Sancerre), Sauvignon Gris (from the Southwest), Mauzac rose and white, and Verdanel (from Gaillac) for the white Néphèle cuvée; and 4 ha of Malbec, Cabernet Franc, Prunelard, Cot à Pied Rouge, and Négrette for the black Nigrine cuvée. The plan is to keep the domain to less than 10 ha. The first vintage of Néphèle was 2017, and the first vintage of Nigrine was 2018. The wines are labeled IGP du Lot.

Mas Del Périé

Le Bourg, 46090 Trespoux Rassiels
+33 5 65 30 18 07
Fabien Jouves
masdelperie@wanadoo.fr
www.masdelperie.com

19 ha; 100,000 bottles [map p. 31]

Fabien Jouves took over the estate, which was planted by his parents, in 2009. They had sold the grapes, but Fabien produces his own wine. To emphasize his focus on terroir, he uses a Burgundy-shape bottle rather than the usual Bordeaux bottle. "We're like a Burgundy domain in Cahors," he says. The label says 'Fabien Jouves - Artisan Vigneron.' Cuvées are distinguished both by origin and by maturation regimes. La Roque comes from brown marl, while Les Escures comes from Kimmeridgian limestone; both age in a mix of concrete and barriques. Les Acacias ages in 600-liter demi-muids, Amphore ages in amphora, B763 ages in concrete eggs. All are 100% Malbec. In the range of "terroir wines" there are also Les Pièces Longues (Chenin Blanc from Kimmeridgian limestone aged in wood) and Orange Voilée (an orange wine from Chenin Blanc aged in amphora). In addition there's a large range of red and white entry-level wines.

Métairie Grande du Théron

Le Théron, 46220 Prayssac
+33 5 65 22 41 80
Sébastien Sigaud
barat.sigaud@wanadoo.fr
parcelledesorigines.com

38 ha; 250,000 bottles [map p. 31]

The winery has buildings of yellow stone, with a striking tower, around a central courtyard, in the center of vineyards on the third terrace, overlooking the river Lot. Jean-Marie (at one point the president of the growers' association) and Liliane Sigaud have been in charge since 1973, with their sons Sébastien and Pierre now taking over. The winery was renovated in the 1980s. The flagship is a 100% Malbec, Cuvée Prestige. There are also two special cuvées. Parcelle des Origines A822 comes from a tiny (0.4 ha) plot, where the soil is a think layer of flint and clay on top of limestone. Causse du Theron is made in association with Mendoza producer Altos Las Hormigos, also focusing on expressing limestone through monovarietal Malbec.

Château Pineraie

46700 Puy l'Évêque
+33 5 65 30 82 07
Anne & Emmanuelle Burc
info@chateaupineraie.com
www.chateaupineraie.com

50 ha
[map p. 31]

The estate has been in the Burc family for a very long time—records show them owning land here in 1456—and this is one of the older domains in the appellation, one of the first to start estate-bottling. Anne and Emmanuelle are the sixth generation to make wine. Vineyards are on the second and third terraces, and the calcareous plateau, with plantings of 85% Malbec and 15% Merlot. There are four cuvées in Cahors. The two blends are Cuvée des Dames, which comes from young vines, and ages in cuve, and the estate Château Pineraie, which ages in barriques with 20% new oak. There are two mono-varietal Malbecs: Le Malbec du Château comes from 4 ha on the calcareous plateau, and ages in barriques with 30% new oak; and l'Authenthique du Château Pineraie comes from 5 ha of 100-year-old vines on the third terrace, and ages in barriques for 18% with 70% new oak. There are also rosé and white.

Château Ponzac

46140 Le Causse, Carnac-Rouffiac
+33 6 07 86 49 43
Matthieu Molinié
chateauponzac@wanadoo.fr
www.chateau-ponzac.fr

22 ha; 60,000 bottles
[map p. 31]

The Molinié family have been in the village of Car-nac-Rouffiac since the fourteenth century. Matthieu took over the estate in 1998 with 29 ha and added some plots; the vineyards now have examples of all the local soil types. Matthieu has moved increasingly towards producing lots from individual terroirs. There are five cuvées. Les Peyrières is 100% Malbec from clay in the valley and pebbles on terrace 2, while Château Ponzac is 100% Malbec from clay-limestone. Both age 15% in barriques and 85% in cuve. Maintenant ou Jamais has 95% Malbec and 5% Merlot, coming from marl and limestone and ages in cuve. La Tempéradou is 100% Malbec from the iron-rich sidérolithique soils and ages in barriques; Cot en Dolia also comes from iron-rich clay soils. In addition to the reds, there are whites from Chenin Blanc, Chardonnay, and Viognier.

Domaine du Prince

46140 Saint Vincent Rive d'Olt
+33 5 65 20 14 09
Didier & Bruno Jouve
contact@domaineduprince.fr
www.domaineduprince.fr

27 ha
[map p. 31]

The Jouves have grown vines here for more than three hundred years, sending grapes to the coop until Jacques Jouves started to bottle wine in 1971. Today the domain is presently run by his sons Didier (manager) and Bruno (winemaker). Vineyards are all around the village of Cournou, and have now moved to 100% Malbec. Vinification is traditional, lasting about 4 weeks in stainless steel; then the domain wine is aged in vat, while the cuvée Fut de Chêne ages in wood. There are two special cuvées: Lou Prince, introduced in 2000, comes from a 2 ha plot, and is aged in barrique; and in 2005, cuvée Rossignal was added as a counterpart to Lou Prince, but aged in vat. Causse des Ons is a cuvée intended to express limestone, made in association with Mendoza producer Alto Los Hormigos.

Château Quattre

46800 Bagat-en-Quercy
+33 5 55 86 90 06
Luc Leherle
quattre@vignoblesdeterroirs.com
quattre.vignoblesdeterroirs.com

17 ha; 50,000 bottles
[map p. 31]

Located in the southwest corner of the appellation, on one of the highest terraces, the winery is surrounded by a semicircle of vineyards. Soils are chalky clay, and plantings are 80% Malbec, 15% Merlot, and 5% Tannat. The grape mix of the Cahors cuvée reflects the plantings, and there is also a 100% Malbec, Les Carrals du Château Quattre, which comes from two small parcels of rocky clay-limestone, and ages in 500 liter tonneaux. Château Quattre was purchased in 2008 by the Bordelais negociant, Taillan, which owns Château Chasse Spleen and other properties in Bordeaux.

Les Roques de Cana

Les Roques, 46140 Saint-Vincent-Rive-d'Olt
+33 6 88 92 22 39
Martial Guiette
domainelesroquesdecana@gmail.com
lesroquesdecana.fr

39 ha; 120,000 bottles [map p. 31]

This is a relatively new estate, which Martial Guiette founded in 2003. Religious symbolism runs through the estate, with its name referring to the place where Jesus performed the first miracle. (The village of St. Vincent is named for the patron saint of winemaking.) The purpose-built winery has all the latest equipment. Vineyards are mostly on the Causse, with iron-rich clay-limestone soils facing south. Yields are unusually low for the area. The entry-level wine is cuvée 1305, which ages for 6 months in stainless steel. Le Vin des Noces comes from the third terrace, and ages for 12 months in concrete "to express the freshness and minerality of the terroir." The estate moves into higher gear with two oaked cuvées. Sanguis Christie ages for 14 months in barriques. Le Graal Sanctus comes from 7 ha of the best terroir, and moves into new barriques for malolactic fermentation, followed by aging for 24 months. It is one of the most expensive wines produced in Cahors.

Château de Rouffiac

46700 Duravel
+33 5 65 36 54 27
Pascal Pieron
scea.po.pieron@orange.fr
www.chateau-de-rouffiac.com

75 ha; 400,000 bottles
[map p. 31]

A relatively new domain, the Château de Rouffiac was constructed in the 1980s. Vineyards are planted with Malbec, Merlot, and Tannat, and produce a wide range of cuvées. In monovarietal Malbecs, Seduction comes from gravelly soil, Latitude 44 from iron-rich clay, aged in steel, La Passion from the same terroir but aged in wood, and the top cuvée L'Exception is aged for 24 months in wood. Château Bovila is 80% Malbec and 20% Merlot from limestone terroir, while Prieuré de Bovila is 100% Malbec aged in wood, and Vin Noir du Diable ages longer in wood. Under IGP Côtes du Lot there are also red, white, and rosé.

Domaine des Savarines

Les Savarines, 46090 Trespoux-Rassiels
+33 5 65 22 33 67
Rosie Kindersley
fax +33 5 65 53 11 85

4 ha; 15,000 bottles
[map p. 31]

Danièle Biesbrouck was one of the first involved in the revival of Cahors when she planted the vineyard in 1970 in a 20 ha estate. Thirty years later, in 2003, she sold the estate to Rosie Kindersley and Eric Treuille (who own a bookshop and a butcher in London). (Eric was born in Cahors and apprenticed with a butcher there; Rosie comes from the Kindersley publishing family.) The domaine is located on the Plateau Calcaire above the river Lot and is planted with 4 ha of Malbec and 0.5 ha of Merlot, now about 40 years old. The wine is usually released about five years after the vintage.

Clos Troteligotte

Le Cap Blanc, 46090 Villesèque
+33 6 74 81 91 26
Emmanuel Rybinski
contact@clostroteligotte.fr
www.clostroteligotte.com

16 ha; 80,000 bottles
[map p. 31]

Emmanuel Rybinski has been running this artisanal domain since 1987, returning to polyculture by growing fruits and vegetables, and raising livestock, as well as viticulture. Vineyards are on extremely iron-rich soil on the Plateau Calcaire. K-Nom is the only cuvée to include Merlot (15%) and ages for a year in concrete. All the other cuvées are 100% Malbec. K-Pot is the entry-level wine and ages for 6 months in concrete. K-Or is harvested late and ages for 18 months in concrete vats. K-Lys comes from the plots richest in iron and is harvested early in the season. It ages for 24 months in new barriques. K-2 (named for the mountain) ages in amphora (and gets increased concentration because about 15% evaporates through the clay during 12 months in the clay). There are also Vins de France in all three colors.

Maison Georges Vigouroux

Route de Toulouse, 46003 Cahors
+33 5 65 20 80 80
Bertrand-Gabriel Vigouroux
vigouroux@g-vigouroux.fr
g-vigouroux.fr

150 ha
[map p. 31]

Georges Vigouroux owns several properties in Cahors and the southwest. In Cahors there are Château de Haute-Serre (see mini-profile), Château de Mercuès (a luxury hotel as well as a wine producer with 40 ha of vineyards), and Château Leret-Monpeat. In Buzet there is Château Tournelles. There are also wines under several other labels, including the Vigouroux name itself. Crocus (see mini-profile) is a collaboration with American winemaker Paul Hobbs. The properties in Cahors cover all types of terroir. The less expensive wines are sold under the names of various 'Collections,' gathered together under the name of Atrium. Châteaux de Haute-Serre and Mercuès are the properties with oenotourism, and the ranges of wines run from entry-level to the Icône WOW cuvées.

Château Vincens

Le Foussal, 46140 Luzech
+33 5 65 30 51 55
Philippe Vincens
contact@chateauvincens.fr
www.chateauvincens.fr

30 ha; 250,000 bottles
[map p. 31]

The Vincens family has been in the region for a very long time and bought their first vineyards when Prosper Vincens returned from the First World War in 1919. Grapes were sent to the cooperative until Michel Vincens started to produce wine in 1982. At first it was labeled Domaine des Vincens, before becoming Château Vincens. Michel's children, Philippe and Isabelle, are in charge today. Vineyards are in many small plots. Entry-level wines in red, white, and rosé are IGP Côtes du Lot. The estate Cahors is Malbec aged in cuve; cuvée Prestige is 80% Malbec and 20% Merlot, aged 30% in cuve and 70% in barriques; Origine is 100% Malbec aged in barriques. There are two parcel selections, both 100% Malbec: Le Graves de Paul, which spends 20-22 months in new barriques; and La Parcelle Oubliée which is fermented and then aged in 400-liter barrels.

Domaine Barreau

850 Route de Cordes, 81600 Gaillac
+33 5 63 57 57 51
Sylvain & Romain Barreau
contact@domaine-barreau.com
www.domaine-barreau.com

45 ha; 250,000 bottles
[map p. 36]

Established in 1865, now in its sixth generation, this family estate is located on the slopes a couple of miles from Gaillac, with clay-limestone soils. The entry-level range is called Augustin, aged in cuve, and comes as dry red, rosé, or white, perlé (semis-parkling), or Doux (sweet). Braisers is a step up, aged in oak, and comes as dry red (a blend of Fer Servadou and Syrah) or white (100% Mauzac) or Doux (including some botrytis). The Ancestral range is red or sweet. The red is a blend of Fer Servadou, Prunelart, and Syrah, aged in barriques of new oak; the domain recommends decanting it two hours before drinking. The Doux is a blend of Loin de l'Oeil, Muscadelle, and Mauzac from 50-year old vines, made when conditions allow.

Clos Rocailleux

Lieu dit Condomines, 81140
Andillac
+33 6 80 53 61 16
Luc Bon
luc.bontemps@free.fr
closrocailleux.com

7.5 ha; 25,000 bottles
[map p. 36]

Jack & Margaret Reckit left London in 2011 to buy this estate, where they focused on the indigenous grapes of Gaillac. Luc Bontemps bought the estate in January 2020. The domain is located at about 300m elevation on a limestone plateau. Vines occupy about half the estate, in nine separate parcels. Black plantings are Duras, Fer Servadou, and Syrah; whites are Mauzac, Loin de l'Oeil, and Muscadelle. The Classique red is Syrah and Fer Servadou, aged in cuve; the Reserve also has a little Duras and ages in barriques. The Classique white is a blend of Loin de l'Oeil and Mauzac. Far from the Eye is 100% Loin de l'Oeil, and the Reserve Blanc is 100% Mauzac from 70-year old vines. The whites are made in stainless steel.

L'Enclos des Braves

RD 18, à Vertus, 81800 Rabastiens
+33 6 08 30 27 81
Nicolas Lebrun
contact@lenclosdesbraves.com
www.lenclosdesbraves.com

8 ha
[map p. 36]

Nicolas Lebrun was an oenologist, before he bought a 6 ha vineyard, built a winery, and created the estate with his wife Chantal in 2005. The single block of vineyards is on clay-calcareous soils on the slopes on the right bank of the Tarn southwest of the town of Gaillac. Nicolas focuses on the indigenous varieties of the area. The original estate had 3 ha of black varieties, Duras, Fer Servadou (Braucol), and Gamay, planted in 1976, and 3 ha of white, Loin de l'Oeil and Sauvignon Blanc, planted in 1992. Nicolas planted another 2 ha of Prunelard, Fer Servadou, and Mauzac in 2013. The whites, both dry and sweet, are blends of Sauvignon Blanc and Loin de l'Oeil; the reds are blends of Fer Servadou and Duras or Fer Servadou and Prunelard. Bravissimo comes from old vines of Fer Servadou, and ages in barriques.

Domaine Laubarel

Laubarel Boissel, 81600 Gaillac
+33 5 63 57 41 90
Lucas Merlo
lucas.merlo545@orange.fr
domaine-laubarel.com

7 ha; 35,000 bottles
[map p. 36]

Lucas Merlo, who comes from Albi and wanted to return to his native region, worked in the Médoc and then in Cahors for seven years before buying this property in 2008. Originally founded in 1904, just outside the town of Gaillac, the small domain has a single block of vineyards that includes all the local varieties, planted on clay-calcareous soils. The wines are divided into two ranges. La Cuvée Domaine has blends that come in red, white, rosé and sweet white, all aged in vat. La Cuvée L'Aubarèl has a series of monovarietal wines, with reds from Braucol and Duras, and whites from Mauzac and Len de L'El, all aged in barriques.

Château Montels

Burgal, 81170 Souel
+33 5 63 56 01 28
Bruno Montels
brmontels@gmail.fr
brunomontels.com

25 ha
[map p. 36]

Bruno Montels took over part of the family vineyards and created the domain in 1985, initially under the name Domaine Saint André. He built the winery in 1991 and extended it in 1997 and 2003. His daughter Marie joined the domain in 2018. Located on the calcareous plateau of Cordes, northeast of the town of Gaillac, the domain makes a range or dry red and dry and sweet white wines. The red l'Esprit de Terroir is a blend of Fer Servadou, Syrah, and Merlot; Les Trois Chênes and Le Secret de Saint André are Fer Servadou and Syrah. The whites are blends of Mauzac, Sauvignon, Muscadelle, and Loin de l'Oeil. The Vendange Tardive comes from parcels of Muscadelle, and Loin de l'Oeil in the Cérou valley where morning mist is common to generate botrytis. There are also Chardonnay and Pinot Noir labeled as Vin de France.

Domaine du Moulin

Chemin des Crêtes, 81600 Gaillac
+33 5 63 57 20 52
Nicolas Hirissou
contact@ledomainedumoulin.com
www.ledomainedumoulin.com

40 ha; 140,000 bottles [map p. 36]

This family domain originated in 1827. Jean-Paul and Dominique Hirissou took over in 1976, and handed over to their son Nicolas in 2002. Jean-Paul, who still manages the vineyards, sold the grapes, and Nicolas started estate bottling. Half the vineyards are on the left bank of the river Tarn, on gravelly soils, and the other half on the right bank with clay-calcareous soils. Some of the vineyards were planted in 2005 with the unusually high vine density for the region of 7,500 plants/ha. Nicolas feels this makes a great difference to the quality. The Gaillac red is an equal blend of Syrah and Duras; Cuvée Florentin is 100% Braucol, aged in barriques. Under IGP Côtes du Tarn, Cuvée le Faucon is a blend of 25% Braucol with 75% Tannat. The dry whites are blends of local varieties; the top sweet white, Cette Année La, is blend of Chardonnay and Muscadelle, concentrated by passerillage, and labeled as IGP Côtes du Tarn. A sparkling white is made by Méthode Ancestrale.

Domaine Rotier

Petit Nareye, 81600 Cadalen

+33 5 63 41 75 14

Alain Rotier

rotier.marre@domaine-rotier.com

www.domaine-rotier.com

35 ha; 150,000 bottles [map p. 36]

Established in 1975, when Gérard and Michèle Rotier purchased the estate, the domain started estate-bottling when their son Alain joined in 1985. Alain's brother-in-law Francis Marre joined in 1997, and today Francis manages the vineyards and Alain makes the wine. Plantings are 25 ha of black varieties and 10 ha of white, with the focus on indigenous varieties Duras for reds and Loin de l'Oeil for whites. The domain is especially known for its doux (sweet) wine, which is 80% Loin de l'Oeil and 20% Sauvignon Blanc, and usually has 90 g/l residual sugar. The botrytized Vendange Tardive, Renaissance, is 100% Loin de l'Oeil, and has 185 g/l residual sugar; it ages in barriques of oak and acacia for 10 months. The dry white, Les Gravels, is 85% Loin de l'Oeil and 15% Sauvignon Blanc, aged in cuve. Esquisse is 85% Loin de l'Oeil and 15% Sauvignon Blanc, and has no added sulfur. Reds have 45-90% Duras, blended with Fer Servadou, Syrah, Prunelard, and Cabernet Sauvignon. Les Gravels ages in cuve, Esquisse ages in cuve with no added sulfur, Renaissance ages in barriques with 15% new oak, and L'Ame ages in new barriques.

Domaine des Terrisses

81600 Gaillac

+33 5 63 57 16 80

Alain & Brigitte Cazottes

gaillacterrisses@orange.fr

domainedesterrisses.com

40 ha [map p. 36]

Located on the clay-limestone slopes overlooking the town of Gaillac, the domain has been in the Cazottes family since 1750. Alain took over in 1984 and is the seventh generation. (The name, Terrisses, refers to the bricks made from the local clay that were used to construct the buildings.) The focus in the vineyards is on the traditional local varieties, divided into 25 ha with black varieties (Braucol, Duras, and the rare Prunelart) and 15 ha with white varieties (Mauzac and Loin de l'Oeil). Terrisses is used to describe the entry-level range, and Terre Originelle is a higher level. The Terrises red is a blend of Duras, Bracol, Syrah, and Prunelart, aged in cuve, while the Terre Originelle is 85% Braucol and 15% Prunelart, aged in barriques with 20% new oak. There are both dry and sweet whites. The dry Terrisses is 40% Loin de l'Oeil, 40% Mauzac, and 20% Sauvignon Blanc, while Terre Originelle is 60% Loin de l'Oeil and 40% Sauvignon Blanc, aged in cuve with battonage to add richness. The medium-sweet whites come from 100% Mauzac, with old vines used as the source for Terre Originelle. A sparkling wine made by the ancestral method (a single fermentation in the bottle) comes from Mauzac. There's also a special cuvée, variously called either Le Monde en Parle or L'Orée des Terrisses, which is a monovarietal made from whichever variety does best each vintage.

Fronton

Château Baudare

161, rue Basse-Près-de-l'Église,
82370 Campsas

+33 5 63 30 51 33

Claude & David Vigouroux

vigouroux@aol.com

chateaubaudare.com

80 ha
[map p. 36]

Jean Vigouroux was making wine in the region in 1820. The estate was created in 1882 when his son Léon purchased the first vines at Campsas. David Vigouroux took over the family domain in 2000. The domain expanded to its present size by the purchase in 2009 of the 20 ha of Domaine Callory. The domain is committed to the local variety Negrette, which is about half of the blend in the Cuvée Prestige (with 50% Cabernet Sauvignon), Secret des Anges (with 40% Syrah and 20% Malbec), Sélection (with 30% Cabernet Sauvignon and 290% Syrah), and Vieilles Vignes (with 50% Syrah, from 40-year-old vines). Perle Noire is 100% Negrette. Most of the wines age in cuve. Haut Expression is 80% Negrette with 10% each of Syrah and Malbec, and ages in barriques. There is also a Syrah. There are several rosés, also consisting of blends based on Negrette. Whites are mostly varietal, from Muscat, Sauvignon Blanc, or Sémillon.

La Colombière

190, route de Vacquiers (D63d),
31620 Villaudric
+33 5 61 82 44 05
Philippe & Diane Cauvin
vigneron@chateaulacolombiere.com
chateaulacolombiere.com

15 ha; 60,000 bottles
[map p. 36]

The domain was created in 1970 by Jean-René Chabanon, who was a follower of Jules Chauvet in Beaujolais (practicing semi-carbonic maceration). François de Driésen bought the domain in 1984; his daughter Diane, and her husband Philippe Cauvin, took over in 2006. The focus is on Negrette, which is the basis of most of the cuvées. Bellouguet is a blend of Negrette and Cabernet Franc, Façon Puzzle is Negrette and Syrah, and Coste Rouge is varietal Negrette. From Negrette there are also clairet (light red), vin gris (rosé), and a sparkling wine. The Cauvins also found some examples of the pre-phylloxera white variety Bouysselet, and grafted it on to two parcels, from which they make the Grand B varietal cuvée and the blend with Chenin Blanc and Sauvignon Blanc of Les Jacquaires, both Vin de France.

Château Montauriol

1925 Route des Châteaux, 31340 Villematier
+33 5 61 35 30 58
Nicolas & Catherine Gelis
contact@chateau-montauriol.com

35 ha
[map p. 36]

Nicolas Gelis started making wine in 1994 when he purchased Château Ferran, an abandoned property in Fronton. In 1998 he purchased the 90 ha estate of Château Montauriol with its eighteenth century château. In 2008, he added Château Cahuzac to the portfolio. As Château Montauriol has a modern winery, the wines are made here. From its 25 ha, Château Ferran makes lighter, fruity wines. The vineyards at Château Montauriol fall into two groups: there are 15 ha of clay-based soils on the plain, while 20 ha of terraces have iron-rich gravelly soils. Montauriol produces weightier wines, from blends of Negrette with Syrah and Cabernet Franc. In addition to the Cuvée Tradition, aged in cuve, the cuvées Prestige and Mons Aureolus are aged in barrique.

Madiran

Domaine Berthoumieu

1352 Chemin Estredembat, lieu-dit Dutour, 32400 Viella
+33 5 62 69 74 05
Claire & Marion Bortolussi
contact@domaine-berthoumieu.com
www.domaine-berthoumieu.com

25 ha; 160,000 bottles
[map p. 41]

The domain was founded in the 1850s, and acquired a high reputation after Didier Barré purchased it in the 1990s. It was sold in 2016 to Claire and Marion Bortolussi, daughters of Alain Bortolussi at Château de Viella (see mini-profile). Vineyards have two distinct terroirs: clay-stony facing south, and clay-flinty facing east. Plantings are mostly black varieties; there are 3 ha of whites. There are three red wines from Madiran: Charles de Batz (named after Musketeer D'Artagnan) is 90% Tannat and 10% Cabernet Sauvignon from 50-100-year old vines on stony clay; Haut Tradition is 60% Tannat, 30% Cabernet Sauvignon, and 10% Pinenc, from 20-50-year old vines on flinty, stony, clay; and Rouge

Pointé is 50% Tannat, 35% Cabernet Sauvignon, and 15% Cabernet Franc from younger vines on more gravelly soil. All age in barriques. In the best years, Didier Barré used to make a cuvée called MCM from Tannat planted in 1900. Dry and sweet whites are blends from Gros and Petit Manseng, and Courbu, and are labeled as Pacherenc du Vic-Bilh. Tanatis is a fortified sweet wine made from Tannat.

Domaine Chapelle Lenclos

Château d'Aydie 64330 Aydie
+33 5 62 69 78 11
Famille Laplace
contact@famillelaplace.com
www.famillelaplace.com

65 ha; 600,000 bottles

Patrick Ducournau is famous for inventing the technique of micro-oxygenation that's widely used to tame the tannins of Tannat. He owns two domains, Mouréou and Chapelle Lenclos. Domaine Mouréou is a blend of 70%Tannat and 30% Cabernet Sauvignon, aged in vats and oak for 24 months. In effect, Chapelle Lenclos is the top cuvée of the combined operation and is 100% Tannat, aged for 12 months in barriques followed 12 months in vat. Since 2005, the wines have been made by his cousins at Vignobles Laplace, and Patrick continues to work on the technology of vinification. The wines can be tasted at Château d'Aydie.

Cave de Crouseilles

Route de Madiran, 64350
Crouseilles
+33 5 59 68 57 14
Roland Podenas
info@crouseilles.fr
crouseilles.com

700 ha; 5,000,000 bottles
[map p. 41]

The Cave de Crouseilles was created in 1950. It now includes 130 growers, and represents a third of the production of Madiran and Pacherenc du Vic-Bilh. Around 80% of the vineyards are used for Madiran. In 1979, the coop bought the Château de Crouseilles, which had become dilapidated, replanted the vineyards, and resumed production in 1986. It's now used for an entry-level Madiran. In 1999, the Cave de Crouseilles joined the Plaimont cooperative (see mini-profile), making it part of the largest producer in the southwest. The styles of Madiran extend from Nouveau (from young vines, with less extraction, some use of thermovinification, and other techniques to make the wine more immediately approachable) to Classique (mostly aged in cuve but with a proportion in barrique). The blend is Tannat, Cabernet Sauvignon, and Cabernet Franc. The cooperative was restricted to large scale production until it bought the cellars of Château Arricau-Bordes in 2001 and Château de Diusse in 2012, giving it the ability to vinify small parcels. This is used to produce the Vignobles Marie Maria range, which has cuvées representing individual places or terroirs, such as Argilo for clay-limestone, Grevière for gravelly-clay soils found at mid-slope, and Veine for pebbly terroir at the highest altitudes.

Domaine Labranche Laffont

32400 Maumusson
+33 5 62 69 74 90
Christine Dupuy
christine.dupuy@labranchelaffont.fr

22 ha; 100,000 bottles
[map p. 41]

Christine Dupuy took over this family domain when her father died in 1992; she had just graduated from oenology school, and the estate was only 6 ha. Plantings are mostly black, and include some very old Tannat vines planted before phylloxera. There are 3 ha of Gros and Petit Manseng for the whites. Madiran Tradition is 70% Tannat with 15% each of Cabernet Sauvignon and Cabernet Franc, aged one third in barriques. The Vieilles Vignes cuvée is 100% Tannat from vines more than 60-years old. Cuvée Les Préphylloxériques comes from the very old Tannat vines. The dry white Pacherenc du Bic-Bilh is 70% Gros Manseng and 30% Petit Manseng and is aged in barriques. Christine is widely considered to have made the point that Tannat does not need to be rustic.

Château Laffitte Teston

32400 Maumusson
+33 5 62 69 74 58
Jean Marc Laffitte
info@laffitte-teston.com
www.chateau-laffitte-teston.com

42 ha; 220,000 bottles
[map p. 41]

Considered to be an ambassador for the region, Jean Marc Laffitte established the reputation of this family domain, and now his children Joris et Erika, the sixth generation, are involved. From Madiran, the cuvée Reflet du Terroir is 80% Tannat with 10% each of Cabernet Sauvignon and Cabernet Franc, and ages in 1- and 2-year barriques. Vieilles Vignes comes from 70-year old Tannat, and ages in new barriques. Erika is the dry Pacherenc du Vic-Bilh and is 70% Petit Manseng, 20% Gros Manseng, and 10% Petit Corbu. Rêve d'Automne is moelleux, and almost entirely Petit Manseng. There are also wines labeled by varietal names under IGP Côtes de Gascogne.

Domaine Laffont

32400 Maumusson
+33 5 62 69 75 23
Pierre Speyer
info@domainelaffont.fr
www.domainelaffont.fr

12 ha; 20,000 bottles
[map p. 41]

This domain is a little unusual in having more white plantings than black. The original vineyards consist of 4 ha planted with 80% Tannat and some Cabernet Franc and Petit Manseng. Nearby, another 8 ha are planted with Petit Manseng, Gros Manseng, and Petit Courbu. All the Madiran cuvées age in barriques. Tradition is a blend of Tannat with Cabernet Franc, and Erigone is 100% Tannat. More intense, Hecate is 100% Tannat aged in new barriques. Céleste is produced only in top years. There are both dry and sweet cuvées from Pacherenc. The dry wine has Gross and Petit Manseng and Petit Courbu; the sweet wine has only Petit an Gros Manseng. Both age in barriques (new for the dry wine).

Domaine Laougué

Route de Madiran, 32400 Viella
+33 5 62 69 90 05
Pierre Dabadie
geoff@deconcept.com
www.domaine-laougue.fr

22 ha
[map p. 41]

Pierre Dabadie took over this old family domain in 1980, when it had only 7 ha. He expanded the holdings, and the majority of vineyards (18 ha) are in Madiran. His son Sylvain took over in 2014. The Madiran cuvée Camy comes from 50% Tannat with 25% each of Cabernet Sauvignon and Cabernet Franc grown on south-facing slopes, and ages for a few months in 1- and 2-year barriques. Cuvée Marty has 80% Tannat with 10% of each Cabernet, and ages for a year in new barriques. The dry white Classique from Pacherenc is a blend of Petit and Gros Manseng; and Passion de Charles is a dry white, 100% Courbu, aged in barriques with a third new oak. The moelleux Pacherenc du Vic-Bilh is an equal blend of Gros and Petit Manseng; cuvée Tradition is doux (sweeter). The top of the line red is Arbison, a 100% Tannat introduced in 2014. The white counterpart, introduced in 2015, is Le Talion, which has 90% Petit Courbu and 10% Petit Manseng. Both age in barriques.

Clos Les Mets d'Âmes

Clos Les Mets D'âMes, Chemin
Lafitau, 64350 Aurions Idernes
+33 5 59 12 00 80
Céline Oulié
contact@lesmetsdames.com
lesmetsdames.com

9 ha
[map p. 41]

Céline Oulié created the Mets d'Âmes in 2014. The 30 ha estate is in a single block, with 6,5 ha of black grape varieties, just over 1 ha of white grape varieties, 16 ha planted with cereals, and uncultivated areas of open land and woods. She is committed to production of natural wines, under the new appellation description of Vins Naturels from Madiran and Pacherenc du Vic-Bilh. An old stable was converted to a winery. Wines have somewhat funky names and labels reflecting the approach. L'Ove is a dry white from equal proportions of Petit Courbu and Gros Manseng, aged in concrete eggs, Les Sens de le Vie is an entry-level red from 75% Tannat and 25% Cabernet Sauvignon, aged in concrete and in foudre. Réchauffement du Climax is 100% Tannat, aged in foudre. Two might entry-level wines are Vins de France, the red Pimpren'elle red and the off-dry white Les Oeufs Plus Gros Que le Ventre. Oenotourism offers tours of the estate as well as tastings.

Domaine du Moulié

32400 Cannet
+33 5 62 69 77 73
Lucie et Michèle Charrier
domainedumoulie@orange.fr
www.domainedumoulie.com

16.5 ha [map p. 41]

'Moulié' means windmill and flour in Gascon, and implies that the domain might be on the site of an old windmill. The first actual trace of the domain dates from 1764, when it had 20 ha and was producing red wine from 3 ha. The Chiffre family purchased the property in 1920. Wine was sold in bulk until estate-bottling started in 1981. Sisters Lucie and Michèle took over in 2002; Lucie is the winemaker, and Michèle manages the vineyards. Today the estate of 70 ha includes 15 ha devoted to Madiran and 1.5 ha for Pacherenc du Vic Bilh (certified organic). Moulié is the first Madiran cuvée, 80% Tannat and 20% Cabernet Franc, aged in cuve; Chiffre is 100% Tannat and ages in a mix of one-year and two-year barriques. L'Insolite is the first Pacherenc; 45% Arrufiac, 45% Petit Courbu, and 10% Petit Manseng, it ages in cuve. Selected by successive passes through the vineyard, Pouymarie is 54% Arrufiac and 46% Gros Manseng, also aged in cuve. Cuvée 'L' is all Manseng, 98% Petit Manseng and 2% Gros Manseng, and ages in barriques.

Château Peyros

9 Chemin du Château, 64350
Corbère-Abères
+33 5 59 68 10 51
Arnaud Lesgourgues
chateau.peyros@leda-sa.com
maison-leda.com

22 ha; 130,000 bottles

Jean Jacques Lesgourgues bought Château Peyros in 1999. The Lesgourgues family also started Maison Lèda, which distributes Château Peyros, several Bordeaux châteaux, and producers of Armagnac, Cognac, Calvados, and other spirits. Château Peyros is almost off the map of Madiran, located at the absolute far south of the appellation, with vineyards on south-facing slopes. Peyros means stony place in Gascon, and the terroir consists of pouzzolanes, a conglomerate consisting of galets surrounded by in clay. Plantings are 70% Tannat and 30% Cabernet Franc. Vinification focuses on softening the tannins of Madiran, with micro-oxygenation after alcoholic fermentation, and some malolactic fermentation in barriques. Tradition is 60% Tannat and 40% Cabernet Franc, and ages in barriques for a year with 25% new oak, while the Vieilles Vignes comes from 40-50-year old vines of 80% Tannat and 20% Cabernet Franc, aging in barriques with 40% new oak for a year.

Cave des Producteurs de Plaimont

32400 Saint Mont
+33 5 62 69 62 87
André Dubosc
vdufau@plaimont.fr
www.plaimont.com

5300 ha; 40,000,000 bottles
[map p. 41]

This very large cooperative was formed by merging several coops in the 1970s. Located just south of Armagnac, it represents more than 800 growers in various appellations, with Saint Mont as its flagship. It is most famous for its Vignes Préphylloxeriques, a cuvée from a small parcel of vines planted in 1871 on sandy soil just above the village of Saint Mont. The vines are mostly Tannat, but include other black and white varieties, some previously unknown. Until 2011, the grapes went into other cuvées, but since then have been made as a separate cuvée of 1,500 bottles each year. Other cuvées from old vines around Saint Mont include La Madeleine, from one of the first parcels replanted after phylloxera. The top dry white is Le Faîte Blanc (AOP Saint Mont), and the top sweet white is Saint Sylvestre (Pacherenc du Vic-Bilh).

Château du Pouey

32400 Viella
+33 6 31 82 96 91
Bastien Lannusse
ch.pouey@orange.fr
www.chateau-du-pouey.com

22 ha; 45,000 bottles [map p. 41]

The name of the domain means 'hill,' and the winery offers a view over the vineyards. Pierre Bastien started with 2 ha and increased the domain to its present size. His son Bastien took over in 2012 and moved to estate-bottling. Madiran Tradition is 60% Tannat, 20% Cabernet Franc, and 20% Cabernet Sauvignon . Madiran Réserve du Vigneron is 85% Tannat, 10% Cabernet Franc, and 5% Cabernet Sauvignon. Madiran Bastien is 100% Tannat, and ages in barriques. There are both dry and sweet whites from Pacherenc, and a rosé from Côtes de Gascogne.

Domaine Sergent

32400 Maumusson
+33 5 62 69 74 93
Corinne Dousseau
contact@domaine-sergent.com
www.domaine-sergent.com

21 ha; 120,000 bottles
[map p. 41]

The Dousseau family purchased this domain in 1902; Gilbert Dousseau handed over to his daughters Brigitte and Corinne in the late nineties. Cuvée Tradition has 80% Tannat and 10% each of Cabernet Sauvignon and Cabernet Franc, and is softened by micro-oxygenation. The cuvée Elevé en Fûts de Chêne, is 100% Tannat, and as its name indicates, ages in barriques. Less than 1,000 bottles are produced of the top wine, called Cuvée Eucalyptus, which is 100% Tannat aged in 400-liter barrels for two years. In whites, the dry Pacherenc du Vic-Bilh Sec is half each of Petit and Gros Manseng. In sweet wines, the Doux cuvée is a blend of both varieties, and Grains d'Elise is harvested very late from the best parcels, mostly Petit Manseng.

Stratéus

7, imp. Congalinon, 65700 Madiran

+33 6 76 54 13 21

Simon Ribert

strateus.madiran@gmail.com

www.strateus-madiran.com

3 ha

[map p. 41]

The smallest domain in the appellations, this has 1.15 ha in Madiran and 2 ha in Pacherenc. It was created in 2017 when Simon Ribert's grandfather gave him parcels of 80-year-old vines, south-facing on the slopes around the town of Madiran. Simon spent a year working at Château Montus before setting out on his own. The wines were initially made at the cooperative. Black varieties, two thirds Tannat and one third Cabernet Franc, are planted on pebbly soils of white and black clay, and white varieties, two thirds Petit Manseng and one third Gros Manseng, are planted on clay and gravel. There is one red Madiran cuvée, and both dry and sweet whites (the latter from young vines that Simon planted) from Pacherenc.

Château de Viella

Route de Maumusson, 32400 Viella

+33 5 62 69 75 81

Alain Bortolussi

contact@chateauviella.fr

www.chateauviella.fr

25 ha; 150,000 bottles

[map p. 41]

The Bortolussi family has owned this domain since 1952. Alain is the third generation, and replanted and expanded the vineyards after he took over in 1990. The ruined eighteenth century château was restored in 2005. His daughters bought nearby Domaine Berthoumieu (see mini-profile) in 2016. Plantings at Château de Viella are 80% black varieties. There are three red cuvées: Madiran Tradition is 60% Tannat and 40% Cabernet Franc, from younger vines on gravelly soil, aged one third barriques; Expression is 80% Tannat and 20% Cabernet Sauvignon from 25-year-old vines on stony-clay, aged in barriques; and Prestige is 100% Tannat, aged in new barriques. Dry and sweet whites under the Pacherenc du Vic-Bilh label are blends from Gros and Petit Manseng, and Arrufiac. Vinosolis is a fortified sweet wine from Tannat.

Jurançon

Domaine Bayard

30 Chemin Pierrette, 64360 Monein

+33 6 20 58 43 20

Rose & Louis Laborde

laborde.bayard@gmail.com

domaine-bayard-jurancon.fr

3 ha

[map p. 45]

This tiny domain — 6 ha in total, with half planted to vines, with an average age of 30 years — was bought by Rose and Louis Laborde in 2016. They built a new wood-paneled tasting room in 2019. They produce two cuvées each of Jurançon Sec and Jurançon, as well as a sparkling wine, Nebula, by Méthode Champénoise from 100% Gros Manseng. The dry Griffe d'Ucha is 60% Petit Manseng and 40% Gros Manseng, aged in cuve, while Papilles d'Ucha is 65% Petit Manseng and 35% Gros Manseng, aged in demi-muids with battonage for 16 months. In Jurançon Doux (sweet), Symbiose is 60% Petit Manseng and 40% Gros Manseng, aged on the lees in stainless steel for 9 months, while Myriades is 100% Petit Manseng, aged in barriques for 16 months.

83

Domaine Bellegarde

Quartier Coos, 64360 Monein
+33 5 59 21 33 17
Pascal Labasse
contact@domainebellegarde-jurancon.com
www.domainebellegarde-jurancon.com

15 ha; 70,000 bottles [map p. 41]

Just outside the village of Monein, the estate dates from the eighteenth century and was acquired by Gratien Labasse in 1920. Estate-bottling started when Pascal took over in 1985. Plantings are 60% Petit Manseng, 36% Gros Manseng, and 4% Camaralet. There are two dry wines from Jurançon. Energique is Gros Manseng and ages in stainless steel; La Pierre Blanche is mostly Petit Manseng and ferments and ages in barriques. In addition, cuvée Unique is from the forgotten variety, Camaralet, labeled as IGP Comte Tolosan. There are four moelleux cuvées. Historique is 80% Petit Manseng (aged in barriques) and 20% Gros Manseng (aged in stainless steel). Thibault is harvested from 9 ha of south-facing Petit Manseng in November and ferments and ages in barriques. La Comète is also Petit Manseng, harvested at the end of October, and fermented and aged in barriques with 20% new oak. Selection DB is harvested at the end of December from two parcels of old vines Petit Manseng, which give very low yields (9 hl/ha). It ferments and ages in new barriques.

64360 Monein
+33 5 59 21 36 34
Claude Loustalot
contact@cdconstructions.com
www.jurancon-bio.com

11 ha; 40,000 bottles
[map p. 45]

Claude Loustalot took over this domain in 1994 from his uncle, Georges Bru-Baché, who was a well-known local figure. Vineyards just outside Monein are on steep terraces facing south to south-east, and are planted with Petit (75%) and Gros Manseng (20%). Jurançon Sec is 100% Petit Manseng and is vinified entirely in steel. The cuvée Les Castérasses is 70% Gros Manseng and 30% Petit Manseng, aged in 2- and 3-year barriques, and moves in a more saline, mineral direction. The sweet *Jurançon tout court* is 100% Gros Manseng, aged in cuve; the sweet Les Castérasses reverses the proportion of the dry white and is 70% Petit Manseng and 30% Gros Manseng, aged in oak. The two richest cuvées are La Quintessence, 100% Petit Manseng, harvested in November and aged for 18 months in 1-year and new barriques, and L'Eminence, a selection of the best lots of Petit Manseng aged in new barriques, made only in top years.

Domaine Burgué-Séré

157 Côte Labiste et Bassot, 64110 Saint-Faust
+33 5 59 83 06 40
Benoît & Sébastien Séré
jeannot.sere@orange.fr
www.juranconburguesere.com

7.5 ha [map p. 45]

Dating from 1807, this family domain is now in its fifth generation under brothers Benoît et Sébastien Séré, who took over from their parents in 2010. The winery and tasting room were renovated in 2018. Vineyards are on the slopes around the village of Saint Faust at 300m altitude. The focus is on Petit Manseng for the two (sweet) Jurançon cuvées, both 100% varietal. Tradition ages in cuve, while La Palombière ages in foudres for 24 months. There is also Jurançon Sec. Red and rosé come from Tannat and Cabernet Sauvignon, and are labeled as IGP.

84

Domaine Castéra

Chemin de Castéra, Quartier
Uchaa, 64360 Monein
+33 5 59 21 34 98
Christian and Franck Lihour
contact@domainecastera.fr
www.domainecastera.fr

12 ha; 45,000 bottles [map p. 45]

The domain has existed since 1750, and the Lihour family bought it in 1885; they are now in the fifth generation under Franck, who took over in 2014. Petit Manseng is half of plantings, Gros Manseng is most of the rest, and there is a little Petit Courbu. Grapes are pressed as whole bunches, and wines age in a mix of stainless steel and wood. The classic cuvées are Jurançon Sec (95% Gros Manseng with a little Petit Manseng and Courbu), and Jurançon (Petit Manseng and Gros Manseng). Franck introduced single-parcel cuvées, the Tauzy Jurançon Sec and the Caubeight Jurançon.

Clos Thou

254 Chemin Larredya, 64110
Jurançon
+33 5 59 06 08 60
Henri Lapouble Laplace
clos.thou@wanadoo.fr
www.clos-thou.com

9 ha; 35,000 bottles
[map p. 45]

Clos Thou is located in one of the best-known areas of the appellation, at Chapelle de Rousse. The name comes from Raymonde de Thou, who owned the property in 1538. The Lapouble Laplace family purchased it three generations ago; Henri Lapouble Laplace took over in 1993. The terroir is the famous Poudingues de Jurançon. Vineyards on the steep hillsides are planted with almost two thirds Petit Manseng and one third Gros Manseng, and a small amount of Petit Courbu and Camalaret. Délice de Thou is used to describe the basic wine for both Jurançon Sec (dry) and Jurançon (sweet). The Jurançon Sec cuvée Guilhouret is fatter. Suprême de Thou is the top sweet wine in the regular moelleux category. Terroir de la Cerisaie is a richer Vendange Tardive.

Clos Uroulat

64 chemin Uroulat, Quartier
Trouih, 64360 Monein
+33 5 59 21 46 19
Charles Hours
contact@uroulat.com
www.uroulat.com

16 ha; 70,000 bottles
[map p. 45]

This family domain is run by father Charles Hours, who purchased the property in 1983, and his daughter Marie, who joined in 2006. They present themselves as producing two ranges of wines: TRADI (traditional) from Charles, and TRENDY (new generation) from Marie. The wines that established the reputation of the domain are the traditional cuvées: Cuvée Marie for dry white from one third Gros Manseng and two thirds Petit Manseng; and the Moelleux (sweet) Uroulat, from Petit Manseng only. Both are barrel-fermented, with 10% new oak for the dry wine and 20% new for the sweet). The Trendy Happy Hours come in dry and sweet cuvées, and are effectively a lower-level addition to the range.

84 of 108

Domaine de Cabarrouy

448 Chemin Cabarrouy, 64290
Lasseube
+33 5 59 04 23 08
Patrice Limousin & Freya Skoda
domaine.cabarrouy@orange.fr
domainedecabarrouy.simdif.com

5.5 ha
[map p. 41]

The name of the domain comes from Arnaud Caparrouy in the seventeenth century, and vineyards have been planted here since the eighteenth century. Patrice Limousin, a young winegrower from Nantes, and Freya Skoda, from Berlin, bought this abandoned domain in 1988. They replanted vineyards, restored the eighteenth century house, and constructed a winery. The estate includes 15.5 ha of prairie and forest as well as the vineyards. Plantings are 60% Petit Manseng and 40% Gros Manseng. The Jurançon Sec is harvested in October from 100% Petit Manseng, and ages in stainless steel. The Classique Moelleux is 85% Gros Manseng and 15% Petit Manseng, while the moelleux cuvée Ambre de Samonios is 100% Petit Manseng; harvested from the end of October through December, both age in stainless steel. The top cuvée is Sainte Catherine, harvested very late from 100% Petit Manseng, and fermented and aged in barriques.

Clos Guirouilh

Route Belair, 64290 Lasseube
+33 5 59 04 21 45
Jean Guirouilh
guirouilh@gmail.com

10 ha; 50,000 bottles [map p. 41]

The estate has been in the family since the sixteenth century, and Jean Guirouilh is the fourth generation of winemakers. Lasseube is located in a valley in the southern part of the appellation. Vineyards are at an average elevation of 350m on calcareous clay, staked individually and trellised high to catch the Foehn wind that dries the grapes and makes the late harvests possible. The Jurançon Sec is 85% Gros Manseng and 15% Courbu, aged in stainless steel; La Peïrine (taking its name from the small rocks in the vineyard) is 50% each of Gros and Petit Manseng, aged in a mix of foudres and barriques. The Jurançon from 75% Gros Manseng and 25% Petit Manseng is picked in October, and ages in old barriques and foudres. Jurançon Vendange Tardive is 70% Petit Manseng and 30% Gros Manseng from older vines, picked between mid November and mid December, and ages in a mix of new and one-year barriques. Petit Cuyalàa has similar harvesting and vinification, but is 100% Petit Manseng from a single plot.

Château Jolys

330 Route de La Chapelle de Rousse,
64290 Gan
+33 5 59 21 72 79
Camille Bessou-Latrille
contact@domaineslatrille.fr
www.domaineslatrille.fr

30 ha; 130,000 bottles
[map p. 45]

In the eastern part of the appellation, just south of Chapelle de Rousse, this is one of the largest domains in Jurançon. Camille and Claire Latrille, the granddaughters of Pierre-Yves Latrille, an agricultural engineer who founded the domain in 1936, took over from their Aunt Marion in 2013. The Jurançon Sec is 60% Petit Manseng and 40% Gros Manseng and ages in steel; Cuvée Pauline is 100% Petit Manseng and ages briefly in barriques. Similarly, the Jurançon is equal Petit and Gros Manseng aged in steel, while Cuvée Jean is 100% Petit Manseng aged in barriques. There are two Vendange Tardive cuvées, The château bottling is 100% Petit Manseng, harvested in mid December, and aged in steel. Cuvée Épiphanie is harvested even later and ages in barriques. Château Jurque is a smaller property (10 ha) close by, created in 2000 when Pierre-Yves and Marion replanted a pasture with vines; it makes a similar range of wines to Château Jolys.

Clos Larrouyat

*129 Chemin de Lannegrand, 64290
Gan*

+33 6 89 27 26 51

Maxime Salharang

maxime.salharang@hotmail.fr

3 ha; 17,500 bottles
[map p. 45]

Maxime Salharang apprenticed at Domaine de Souch (see profile) and started this tiny estate, named after his grandfather, Roger Larrouyat, in 2011. His first vintage in 2014, was a single barrel. The Jurançon Sec is a blend of 70% Petit Manseng and 30% Gros Manseng. Météore ages for 6 months in barrique with battonage. Comète has the same aging protocol but comes from the youngest vines, which Maxime planted in 2011-2012.

Domaine Naba

*17 Chemin Carrère, 64290
Estialescq*

+33 6 30 69 69 78

Mathieu Lacanette-Naba

contact@domaine-naba.fr

www.domaine-naba.fr

5 ha
[map p. 45]

Mathieu Lacanette-Naba and his father planted their first vines in 2008, on family property where the vines had been pulled out thirty years earlier, and created the domain in 2014 when they restored an old grange to be the winery and started to produce wine. Plantings are Gros and Petit Manseng, Courbu, and Lauzet. There is one dry cuvée and two sweet. The Jurançon Sec, Estia, is 70% Gros Manseng, 20% Courbu, and 10% Petit Manseng. The sweet (doux) Brana is Gros Manseng, and the moelleux Milord is Petit Manseng. Wines age in stainless steel for 6-8 months.

Domaine Nigri

*31 chemin Lacoste Quartier
Candeloup, 64360 Monein*

+33 5 59 21 42 01

Jean-Louis Lacoste

domaine.nigri@wanadoo.fr

16 ha; 70,000 bottles
[map p. 45]

The domain dates back to 1685, and the Lacoste family has been here for four generations. The buildings date from the seventeenth century and have been completely restored. In charge since 1993, Jean-Louis Lacoste is known for his modernist approach. Plantings include the old varieties Lauzet and Camaralet as well as Petit and Gros Manseng, although some of the Gros Manseng has now been replaced by Petit Manseng. In sweet wines, Pas de Deux is a blend from 60% Gros Manseng made in cuve and 40% Petit Manseng made in barriques. Toute Une Histoire is 100% Petit Manseng. In dry wines, Pierre de Lune is a blend of 80% Gros Manseng and 20% Petit Manseng. Confluence is Gros Manseng, with 10% each of Lauzet and Camaralet. There is also a Béarn Rouge.

Château de Rousse

*1723 route de la Chapelle de Rousse,
64110 Jurançon*

+33 5 59 21 75 08

Marc & Olivier Labat

chateauderousse@wanadoo.fr

10 ha; 40,000 bottles
[map p. 45]

Located as its name indicates in the top area of Chapelle de Rousse, the estate has been owned by the Labat family for five generations. Brothers Marc and Olivier have been in charge since 2000. The château originated as a hunting lodge for Henri IV, and is just above the horseshoe of terraced vineyards at 330m altitude. The Jurançon cuvée Quatuor is 65% Gros Manseng, 10% Petit Manseng, and 25% Courbu, aged in barriques. Séduction is 100% Petit Manseng, with longer aging in the barriques. The Jurançon Sec (dry white) is 100% Gros Manseng, aged in stainless steel.

Château de Cabidos

64410 Cabidos
+33 5 59 04 43 41
Peggy Alday
contact@chateau-de-cabidos.com
www.chateau-de-cabidos.com

9 ha; 35,000 bottles

The Château originated in the early fifteenth century, was completed in the sixteenth century, partly destroyed during the French Revolution, and then rebuilt. The historic monument stands in its own grounds with a walled garden. Several generations later in 1972, Isabelle and Philippe du Cauzé de Nazelle moved to their ancestral home, restored the château, and planted a vineyard of Petit Manseng, which was replanted in 1995. The château is a few miles north of Pau, and the wines are IGP. A small proportion of Chardonnay and Sauvignon Blanc was introduced. A new winery was built in 2002, and in 2007 Méo Sakorn-Series became the technical director. She introduced a red wine, 100% Syrah, in addition to the dry and sweet cuvées of Petit Manseng. In 2015 the property was purchased by Robert Alday, a magnate from Holland. The entry-level dry white is Le Pic, mostly Sauvignon Blanc and Chardonnay, with a little Petit Manseng. More typical of the region, Cuvée Gaston Phoebus is a Petit Manseng, usually in an off-dry spectrum. There are several medium-sweet cuvées, all from Petit Manseng, with the top wine, L'Or de Cabidos, from a selection of the best lots, made only in the top years. They age in barriques with some new oak.

Irouléguy

Domaine Ameztia

64430 Quartier Germieta, Saint-Étienne-de-Baigorry
+33 6 73 01 27 58
Gexan Costera
ameztia@orange.fr
domaine-ameztia.com

 8 ha

Ameztia means forest in Basque, and the property is an old farm dating from the seventeenth century. Jean-Louis Costera started making wine here in 2001; in 2013 he passed the domain on to his nephew, Gexan, who trained in Bordeaux and was working at Arretxea. Vineyards are in three separate plots, planted with Tannat, Cabernet Franc, and Cabernet Sauvignon for blacks (although Cabernet Sauvignon is slowly being replaced by Cabernet Franc and Tannat), and Gros and Petit Manseng for whites. The estate Irouléguy red is 70% Tannat and 30% Cabernet Franc, aged two thirds in cuve and one third in barriques; intended for longer aging, Artzaina is 90% Tannat and 10% Cabernet Franc, aged for 12 months in foudres. Cuvée Panxto is a cuvée of 60% Cabernet Franc and 40% Tannat from the best plot. The estate white is 70% Gros Manseng and 30% Petit Manseng, aged in a mix of stainless steel and foudres; Artzaina is 60% Gros Manseng and 40% Petit Manseng, aged in foudres. The rosé comes from 50% Cabernet Franc, 20% Cabernet Sauvignon, and 30% Tannat. Eztia is an off-dry wine, where fermentation stops before completion to leave some residual sugar, labeled as Vin de France.

Domaine Arretxea

Bourg, 64220 Irouléguy
+33 5 59 37 33 67
Thérèse & Michel Riouspeyrous
arretxea@free.fr

8 ha

Michel Riouspeyrous's grandfather was a vigneron, but his parents were not interested in producing wine. When he took over in 1990, he started from scratch in viticulture and winemaking. is local dialect for 'house of stone,' a comment on the work involved in creating vineyards here. There's a wide range of cuvées for a small domain. The Irouléguy Rouge is two thirds Tannat with the rest split between Cabernet Sauvignon and Cabernet Franc, aged in cuve, while cuvée Haitza is 70% Tannat and 30% Cabernet Sauvignon, aged in foudres and demi-muids. The rosé is 70% Tannat and 20% Cabernet Sauvignon. Most of the whites are dominated by Gros Manseng with Petit Manseng for the rest and sometimes a little Petit Courbu, but cuvée Grés is 50% Petit Courbu with the rest divided between the two Mansengs. Wines age in foudres, demi-muids, and stainless steel.

Domaine Brana

3 bis Avenue du Jaï Alaï, 64220
Saint Jean Pied de Port
+33 5 59 37 00 44
Jean Brana
brana.etienne@wanadoo.fr
www.brana.fr

22 ha

Pierre-Etienne Brana established a negociant in 1897, his son moved to Saint-Jean-Pied-de-Port, and then in 1984 the Branas were involved resurrecting the appellation when they planted their vineyard in 1984. The white Ilori is an equal blend of % Gros Manseng and Petit Courbu, aged in stainless steel. The red Ohiza is 80% Tannat and 20% Cabernet Franc, aged in 3-year barriques fir 12 months. The Harri Gorri (basque for red stone) is produced by saignée from 70% Tannat and 30% Cabernet Franc. Cuvée Bizi Berri comes from the old varieties Arrouya and Erremaxaoua, with a little Cabernet Franc. There is also a range of eux de vies.

Domaine Etxegaraya

64430 Saint-Étienne-de-Baigorry
+33 5 59 37 23 76
Marianne Hillau
etxegaraya@wanadoo.fr
www.domaine-etxegaraya.fr

7 ha

Located in one of the last villages in France before you cross into Spain, the domain was founded in 1850, and Marianne and Joseph Hillau were the fifth generation when they took over in 1994. After Joseph died in an accident on the steep hillsides, Marianne and her daughter Carolina continued to run the domain. Soils are red sandstone. The Tannat vines are very old, some more than 100 years, and the Cabernet Sauvignon and Cabernet Franc are more recent. The rosé comes from an equal blend of Tannat and Cabernet Sauyignon, while the red is 60% Tannat and 40% Cabernet Franc. Only made in the best years (otherwise blended into the Irrélguy red) Cuvée Lehengoa comes from a single plot and is 80% Tannat from the oldest vines with 20% Cabernet Sauvignon. Cuvée Aitana has the same composition, but ages in foudre.

Domaine Ilarria

Bourg, 64240 Irouleguy
+33 5 59 37 23 38
Peio Espil
ilarria@wanadoo.fr
www.domaine-ilarria.fr
10 ha; 35,000 bottles

The family domain is located in the village. Peio Espil took over in 1988 after getting experience in making Sauternes at La Tour Blanche, and locally at Domaine Cauhapé in Jurançon. Plantings are 2 ha of white and 8 ha of black varieties. The white cuvée is an equal blend of Petit Manseng and Courbu, aged in a mix of stainless steel and wood. The red is a blend of Tannat, Cabernet Franc, and Cabernet Sauvignon, and ages for 12 months in used barriques. Cuvée Bixintxo is made only in top years, and ages for two years in barriques. The red Cuvée Sans Soufre is produced without adding any sulfur.

La Cave d'Irouleguy

Route St Jean Pied de Port, 64430
Saint-Étienne-de-Baigorry
+33 5 59 37 41 33
Olivier Martin
contact@cave-irouleguy.com
www.cave-irouleguy.com

146 ha; 650,000 bottles

Given the difficulties of growing grapes in the region, it is no surprising that the cooperative should be a dominant influence. In fact, the Cave d'Irouléguy represents more than half of the appellation area. Reds and rosés come from Tannat with Cabernet Sauvignon and Cabernet Franc; whites come from Gros and Petit Manseng and Petit Courbu. In addition, there are sparkling wines made by the Méthode Champenoise, and the local aperitif Goxedari, which is made from rosé wine and cherry brandy.

Glossary of French Wine Terms

Classification

There are three levels of classification, but their names have changed:

- *AOP* (Appellation d'Origine Protégée, formerly AOC or Appellation d'Origine Contrôlée) is the highest level of classification. AOPs are tightly regulated for which grape varieties can be planted and for various aspects of viticulture and vinification.
- *IGP* (Indication Géographique Protegée, formerly Vin de Pays) covers broader areas with more flexibility for planting grape varieties, and few or no restrictions on viticulture and vinification.
- *Vin de France* (formerly Vin de Table) is the lowest level of classification and allows complete freedom with regards to varieties, viticulture, and vinification.
- *INAO* is the regulatory authority for AOP and IGP wines.

Producers

- *Domaine* on a label means the wine is produced only from estate grapes (the vineyards may be owned or rented).
- *Maison* on the label means that the producer is a negociant who has purchased grapes (or wine).
- *Negociants* may purchase grapes and make wine or may purchase wine in bulk for bottling themselves. Some negociants also own vineyards.
- *Cooperatives* buy the grapes from their members and make the wine to sell under their own label.

Growers

- There is no word for winemaker in French. The closest would be *oenologue*, meaning a specialist in vinification; larger estates (especially in Bordeaux) may have consulting oenologues.
- A *vigneron* is a wine grower, who both grows grapes and makes wine.
- A *viticulteur* grows grapes but does not make wine.
- A *régisseur* is the estate manager at a larger property, and may encompass anything from general management to taking charge of viticulture or (commonly) vinification.

Viticulture

- There are three types of viticulture where use of conventional treatments (herbicides, insecticides, fertilizers, etc.) is restricted:
- *Bio* is organic viticulture; certification is by AB France (Agriculture Biologique).
- *Biodynamique* is biodynamic viticulture, certified by Demeter.
- *Lutte raisonnée* means sustainable viticulture (using treatments only when necessary). There are various certifications including HVE (Haute Valeur Environmentale).

- *Selection Massale* means that cuttings are taken from the best grape-vines in a vineyard and then grafted on to rootstocks in order to replant the vineyard.
- *Clonal selection* uses (commercially available) clones to replant a vineyard.
- *Vendange Vert* (green pruning) removes some berries during the season to reduce the yield.

Winemaking

- *Vendange entière* means that whole clusters of grapes are used for fermentation.
- *Destemming* means that the grapes are taken off the stems and individual berries are put into the fermentation vat.
- *Fermentation (or Vinification) intégrale* for black grapes is performed in a barrique, standing up open without an end piece. After fermentation, the end is inserted and the wine ages in the same barrique in which it was fermented.
- During fermentation of red wine, grape skins are pushed up to the surface to form a cap. There are three ways of dealing with it:
    - *Pigeage* (*Punch-down*) means using a plunger to push the cap into the fermenting wine.
    - *Remontage* (pump-over) means pumping up the fermenting wine from the bottom of the vat to spray over the cap.
    - *Délestage* (rack-and-return) means running the juice completely out of the tank, and then pouring it over the cap (which has fallen to the bottom of the vat)
- *Chaptalization* is the addition of sugar before or during fermentation. The sugar is converted into alcohol, so the result is to strengthen the alcoholic level of the wine, not to sweeten it.
- A *cuve* is a large vat of neutral material—old wood, concrete, or stainless steel.
- *Cuvaison* is the period a wine spends in contact with the grape skins.
- *Battonage* describes stirring up the wine when it is aging (usually) in cask.
- *Soutirage* (racking) transfers the wine (without the lees) from one barrique to another.
- *Élevage* is the aging of wine after fermentation has been completed.
- *Malo* is an abbreviation for malolactic fermentation, performed after the alcoholic fermentation. It reduces acidity, and is almost always done with red wines, and often for non-aromatic white wines.
- A *vin de garde* is a wine intended for long aging.

Aging in oak

- A *fût* (*de chêne*) is an oak barrel of unspecified size.
- A *barrique* (in Bordeaux or elsewhere) has 225 liters or 228 liters (called a *pièce* in Burgundy).
- A *tonneau* is an old term for a 900 liter container, sometimes used colloquially for containers larger than barriques, most often 500 or 600 liter.
- A *demi-muid* is a 600 liter barrel.
- A *foudre* is a large oak cask, round or oval, from 20-100 hl.

Sweet wines

- *Moelleux* is medium-sweet wine.
- *Liquoreux* is fully sweet dessert wine.
- *Doux* is sweet (usually not botrytized) still or sparkling wine.
- *Mutage* is addition of alcohol to stop fermentation and produce sweet wine. The style is called Vin Doux Naturel (VDN).
- *Passerillage* leaves grapes on the vine for an extended period so that sugar concentration is increased by desiccation.
- *Botrytis*, also known as *noble rot*, means grapes have been infected with the fungus Botrytis cinerea, which concentrates the juice and causes other changes.

92

Index of Estates by Rating

Index of Organic and Biodynamic Estates

Domaine L'Ancienne Cure
Domaine Arretxea
Château Baudare
Domaine Belmont
Domaine Bru-Baché
Domaine la Calmette
Camin Larredya
Domaine de Capelanel
Domaine Castéra
Domaine de Causse Marines
Château du Cèdre
Château de Chambert
Château Champarel
Clos Rocailleux
Clos Thou
Château La Colombière
Combel la Serre
Château Combrillac
Domaine Cosse Maisonneuve
Domaine des Costes
Château Les Croisille
L'Enclos des Braves
Château Feely
Domaine Grande Maison
Château Grinou
Domaine Guirardel
Château Haut Lavigne
Château Haut Monplaisir
Domaine Ilarria
Michel Issaly

Château de la Jaubertie
Domaine Jonc Blanc
Château Kalian
Domaine Labranche Laffont
Château Lacapelle Cabanac
Clos Lapeyre
Domaine Laroque d'Antan
Clos Larrouyat
Mas Del Périé
Clos Les Mets d'Âmes
Château les Miaudoux
Château Monestier la Tour
Château Montus
Domaine du Moulin
Domaine Mouthes Le Bihan
Domaine Nigri
Château le Payral
Château de Peyrel
Domaine Plageoles
Château Ponzac
Les Roques de Cana
Domaine Rotier
Domaine des Savarines
Domaine de Souch
Stratéus
Château Tirecul La Gravière
Château Tour des Gendres
Clos Troteligotte
Château Vari
Château de Cabidos

Index of Estates by Appellation

Jurançon
Domaine Bayard
Domaine Bellegarde
Domaine Bru-Baché
Domaine Burgué-Séré
Camin Larredya
Domaine Castéra
Domaine Cauhapé
Clos Thou
Clos Uroulat
Domaine de Cabarrouy
Domaine Guirardel
Clos Guirouilh
Les Jardins de Babylone
Château Jolys
Clos Lapeyre
Clos Larrouyat
Domaine Naba
Domaine Nigri
Château de Rousse
Domaine de Souch
Madiran
Château Barréjat
Domaine Berthoumieu
Domaine Chapelle Lenclos
Cave de Crouseilles
Domaine Labranche Laffont
Château Laffitte Teston
Domaine Laffont
Domaine Laougué
Vignobles Laplace
Clos Les Mets d'Âmes

Château Montus
Domaine du Moulié
Château Peyros
Cave des Producteurs de Plaimont
Château du Pouey
Domaine Sergent
Stratéus
Château de Viella
Monbazillac
Château Bélingard
Domaine Grande Maison
Château Kalian
Château Montdoyen
Château Tirecul La Gravière
Château Vari
Montravel
Domaine Jonc Blanc
Château Laulerie
Château Moulin Caresse
Château de Peyrel
Château Pique-Sègue
Château Puy Servain
Pécharmant
Château Champarel
Château Les Farcies du Pech
Domaine du Haut-Pécharmant
Chateau Terre Vieille
Château de Tiregand
Saussignac
Château Feely
Château les Miaudoux

Index of Estates by Name

BOOKS by Benjamin Lewin MW

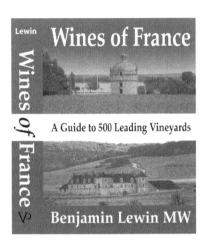

Wines of France

This comprehensive account of the vineyards and wines of France today is extensively illustrated with photographs and maps of each wine-producing area. Leading vineyards and winemakers are profiled in detail, with suggestions for wines to try and vineyards to visit.

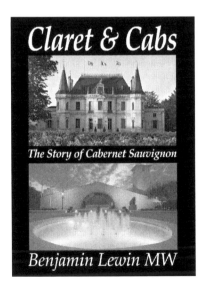

Claret & Cabs: The Story of Cabernet Sauvignon

This worldwide survey of Cabernet Sauvignon and its blends extends from Bordeaux through the New World, defines the character of the wine from each region, and profiles leading producers.

Printed in Great Britain
by Amazon

54094409R00064